A Lifetime Of Experiences For Learning

By

G A Ben Binninger

ISBN:

Paperback 978-1-963764-00-0

Hardback 978-1-963764-01-7

Dedication

This book is dedicated to the caring, decent, and knowledgeable people all over the world who helped make my life all that it has been. Even the not-so-helpful and not-so-nice contributed by showing me what not to do and how not to act.

I also want to dedicate this story to “Prince, “my Maine Coon rescue cat who stayed with me through all this writing, editing, and rewriting, although he did sleep during a lot of the work. Being a southpaw and multi-dexterous like me was valuable, and he contributed significantly to this work with his unwavering support.

My Cat Prince

Contents

Introduction

I started to list many of the fantastic experiences I had in my life, and it seemed the list kept getting longer. After thinking about the contents, I thought it would make sense to remind myself why this happened and how all this came about. This is the result that was most enjoyable to write about and allowed me to relive the experiences and the memories that followed. Of more value are the lessons I learned from these experiences and can share.

My three Sons, Michael, Jon & James

I am blessed with a wonderful life, a great wife, and three terrific boys who have given me delightful grandchildren. I have traveled widely, learned much, accomplished a lot, accumulated some wealth, and made many friends.

This is what happened, why it happened, and some of the fantastic things that happened along the way. I never intended to summarize what I learned, but when I assembled the experiences, advice, notes, stories, talks, and editorials. It seemed to me that this may be helpful to others if put in an organized form, and this is it.

Chapter I

This Is How It All Began

The first step of my journey was spending two years in hospitals until I was five years old. My home away from home was the Hospital for Special Surgery in Manhattan and then Saint Agnus Convalescent Hospital in White Plains, New York, where I recovered from a childhood degenerative hip disease.

The Hospital for Special Surgery New York

While at Saint Agnus, I attended a birthday party for the Lone Ranger's horse Silver. Although confined to my bed like the rest of the kids, I did see the festivities happening in our ward. I have since been on the move to make up for all the lost time. Spending those many hours in a confined space made me highly organized, as I controlled my little part of the world.

Later, I realized my calling was to bring order to things, and in the process, I could do something worthwhile for myself and others. Once out of the hospitals living in New York City, I became a big Yankee fan and was very much into baseball. What I liked about baseball was that if you do not get out, you can keep going.

As I grew up, I realized that the world was not like that. Time is the most limited resource we have and cannot be wasted. Initially, I disliked deadlines; later, I came to like them as they provided a goal and brought closure so I could move on to something else. As a kid in the northeast Bronx, I played in the swamps where the approach to Throgs Neck Bridge was being built. I played in a garbage dump that became a cemetery and ate the crabs I caught with my dad in Zerega Creek, which was infused with waste from a refuse incinerator. When the bridge was built, they mistakenly called it the Throgs Neck Bridge, although the section of the Bronx where I lived is called Throggs Neck. Since I ate everything and lived through all of this, I indeed developed a great immune system and was rarely sick to slow me down.

As a child, I wrote backward with my left hand, so it was not understandable unless someone else held it up to a mirror. The Nuns in grammar school thought this was the sign of the devil and tried everything they could to get me to write right-handed. All they succeeded in was driving me to be quite multi-dexterous.

In the fourth grade, a teacher told me I was too far ahead of the rest of the class, so just be quiet, don't raise my hand, and read a book. However, In the sixth grade, the nun told my mother that I may never get out of grammar school, could not get into a Catholic high school, and college was out of the question. So, I was sent back to the fifth grade. After a week in the fifth grade, that teacher said I should be put back into the sixth grade immediately, and my mom was a lot happier.

My handwriting never improved much, and later in my business career, a boss once remarked, "We all believe that you are brilliant, but no one is sure since we cannot understand your writing." I had no trouble driving on the left side when I lived in England, believing this was the correct way and everyone in the USA had it wrong. Somehow, I saw things a little differently and almost always considered the opposite perspective. Possibly because of this, I tend to look at things from the other person's point of view. This no doubt helped me in my sales and marketing roles. This attribute came in handy in business negotiations by trying to make a bigger pie to share and seeing if there was a way to get something from someone not at the table.

We lived in an Irish-Italian neighborhood. Being Irish, German, and Italian, I could never take sides in the fighting. Since I was both Irish and Italian, I got along with both groups. This probably made me more open and flexible in dealing with others and in my travels to other cultures. My multi-dexterousness helped me learn that changing someone's mind can change their actions, and conversely, changing someone's actions can change their mind.

For some unexplained reason, I was pretty good at many things but was never great at anything. I then realized that change, variety, and accomplishment were my calling rather than excellence or perfection. The upside was that this got me to do a lot and have lots of experiences. I was always organized and tidy and likely had some autism. Once, another boss told me, "No one would keep their office as empty and neat as you because no one would believe that the occupant was doing any work."

My parents had minimal schooling and always impressed me with the importance of getting an excellent education to have the opportunities they never had. It worked for me.

My maternal grandfather was an immigrant who dug graves for a living and did not read, write, or speak English very well. I quickly learned that good communication makes a real difference. There were two important lessons I learned from Mom. I should finish my homework first before I can go out to play and break big problems into smaller ones that are manageable and a lot more.

Getting a Bachelor of Chemical Engineering and a Master in Business degrees helped me in my life and career. However, some of the most important lessons I learned were from my mother when I was a child. Building a sound foundation on some simple principles can enable someone to learn, grow, and accomplish while relating to and working with others.

Chapter II

Mom Helped A Lot

While I learned a lot more from Mom, the following are some of the most valuable lessons. They provided a framework for growth, enrichment, and consideration for me and many others.

Be Nice to People

Show everyone love and kindness. -- Mom was a genuinely lovely person who liked others and was liked by almost everyone. She took the time to show kindness and concern for the people she encountered. She worked in a challenging New York City school cafeteria with some nasty, tough, and difficult kids. While these kids would cause all sorts of trouble, they were always friendly and polite to her as she was to them.

Make sure everyone has enough to eat. -- My family was not wealthy, and when I was young, we did not have a lot. We lived with my grandfather, and mom always took measures to ensure no one went hungry. Mom died of a long and debilitating cancer. When she knew the end was near, she made nearly a year's supply of food for my dad to have after she was gone.

Always arrive with something -- Mom was well-liked and had lots of friends. So, my parents and our family were often invited to people's homes. She always made sure she brought a gift or some food to show her appreciation for the hospitality. I think this is also a good reason she was invited back.

Put family first

While Mom loved everyone, she treasured her family. She only went to work when she found a job in a school cafeteria that allowed her to send my sister and me off in the morning to school yet be home by the time we returned. There was nothing she would not do for Dad and us, no matter what we did. Even though she had late-stage debilitating cancer, her first concern was the family. Her selflessness and caring were virtues that I will always treasure.

You are better

I do not know if I was better than other kids, but to Mom, I was the best. At about the age of three, I spent the next two years away from home in hospitals and a nursing home. Fortunately, after this, I recovered from my illness. Mom always said I was special and could do a lot of great things if I tried. This warm, loving support goes a long way not only in childhood but could carry me through difficult times in adulthood.

Take care of Dad.

While she loved me and my sister, she loved Dad with all her heart. She was the ever-present companion, supporter, and helper. She would do everything she could to make Dad's life better as he did for her. She worried about him more than he needed, but that was her way. Dad passed away at a young age, not many years after Mom. I always believed he died of a broken heart.

Work first, then play later.

When I was in primary school, the kids in the neighborhood went out to play after school. I could not go out with them until my homework was finished. While this was no fun, it taught me discipline and the ability to work very quickly for a goal.

Education will make a better life.

My parents had a limited education. Mom finished the eighth grade while my dad finished only sixth grade to work and support the family during the Depression. My parents regretted the opportunities they never had and drummed into my head not to miss out. They preached that a good education would enable you to learn, grow, achieve, and likely have a better life.

Make measurable and achievable timely goals.

Mom was not a big disciplinarian, and as a matter of fact, she was easygoing. But she wanted me to say what I was going to do and then do it when it was supposed to be done. She was not a taskmaster but someone you did not want to disappoint. Even though the goals were small and short in time, the discipline and habit this created became more powerful than I could have ever imagined as I grew up.

Resilience and Break Big Problems Into Manageable Problems

One of the punishment lessons from school was to write something repeatedly many times. On one occasion, I said to Mom, I could not do this -- it would take forever. She divided the number of times I had to write into a fraction of the work and asked to see how long this took. I did this, and it did not take that long. Then she said all you must do is repeat this correct number of times, and you are done. Making big problems into manageable problems works.

Don't start trouble, but finish it if you must

I grew quickly and was a big kid – nearly six feet and 200 pounds before high school. Mom warned me that if I got into a fight, I would be the one to get in trouble as the bully who started it. So, her advice, which I used, was not to start a fight and try to avoid one. Nonetheless, if it could not be avoided, let the other kid start and do not hold back anything.

Keep at it until it is over.

Even after numerous operations and dashed hopes, Mom lived in faith. She was always an optimist and never gave up fighting. She hung on for years because she wanted to see my sister happily married and to see me graduate from college. I recall coming to the hospital from another state just before she passed away and hearing the doctor say she should not be alive. I guessed she was waiting for me to arrive so all the family could be together at the end.

I know Mom was not perfect, and neither am I. I also know that because of her, I am a better person and that she helped make a better world for those she met.

Chapter III

Growing Up

We lived in the house my grandfather built which was at that time a remote part of the Bronx, NY. My parents bought a house on a lake about 30 miles south of the New York state capital of Albany where my parents were going to retire someday since they never owned their own house. It was a stretch for them to buy this one as they had to cash in their life insurance policies for the money. It was just an unfinished shell at that time. Together, learning from my father, we made this place into a home by adding plumbing, a bathroom, a porch, windows, heating, insulation, electrical and other amenities. This experience taught me to be very handy doing construction crafts and be resourceful in using anything my dad could scavenge. Sadly, they never lived long enough to retire there. This experience ultimately saved me a lot of money and time for the rest of my life by doing things myself.

My parents are buried in Saint Raymond's cemetery near where we lived. When I visited them at the grave, I could see a view of the Empire State Building pointing up to them in heaven.

My early childhood instilled in me a need to learn, a desire to travel, a need to be organized. I found that I acquired the ability to see things differently and to get something accomplished. My Uncle Jimmy was a career Army sergeant who was never in one place for long. He would come to New York every few years to see us and always had great stories and pictures of his travels to Europe, Africa, and Asia, which made me want to see these places.

Later in life, I realized my calling was to figure things out, get things organized and lead the process in the right direction. I was not called upon to run things for a long time, preferring to check the box and move on to the next opportunity.

While I was a kid, my parents bought me my first wristwatch which I broke very soon afterwards. Then they got me another watch, which I broke quickly; I was very active and reckless with a lot of wild playing, and the watches could not survive that. My parents had finished buying me watches, and I had to buy the next watch myself. Yes- I broke this one before very long. From those experiences, I realized I could never wear a watch. So, from that time on, I never wore a wristwatch again (except while running), even in college or while working.

A strange thing happened by not wearing a watch; I developed an amazing sense of keeping track of time. Somehow, I kept track of time in my head without even thinking about it. I was rarely late as I was almost always on time. However, I did wear a watch while running. Although I acquired this excellent sense of time it is only accurate to the minute but not to the second.

My parents provided lots of love, values, encouragement, and skills to go out into the world. I am thankful for all my parents gave me that prepared and motivated me to learn, go, see, and do. This resulted in a fun life while enjoying all the world could offer.

Near where we lived, there was a construction site for new houses; at the site, the workmen drank soda and beer in bottles at lunchtime and left the bottles around the site when they finished working. As a kid, I collected bottles to get money from redemption, and I liked doing something and getting paid for my efforts. After that, I had nine jobs before graduating college, and I learned something important from each.

I sold newspaper subscriptions door to door and learned not to take rejection personally and keep going. I sold food at a concession stand and learned if you are busy the day goes by in a flash. While delivering groceries in lower Manhattan, I quickly found the best way to keep customers happy and, therefore, maximize the tips, which were more than the pay.

Working at a haberdashery store in the south Bronx, I got to see small retail businesses up close and believe everyone should once in their life have a job dealing with the public.

At college, I worked in the electrical engineering lab and learned that research and innovation is slow and tedious. One Christmas, I worked for the Pennsylvania railroad under Penn Station, loading and unloading mail trains. The lesson is that it is better to use your brain than your back, and you will last longer and hold up better. I spent two summers with the New Your Telephone company installing and disconnecting telephones in the Harlem section of the city and learned to go along and get along and never had any problems.

During the summer of my junior year, I worked for Eastman Kodak in Rochester, NY. I got doused with nitric acid, one of the silver refining furnaces that I was studying exploded and since I was working with silver nitrate, my hands got black when exposed to sunlight. These experiences instilled in me the importance of safety, which I have carried forward for all my future jobs and companies. One of which was to take rockets apart for the U.S. Government and deal with ultrahazardous materials- in that role mistakes cannot happen.

Also, much later, after college, in my corporate career, the importance of safety was again reinforced with Hercules, a maker of solid fuel for military rockets and space exploration. The fuels were made in a building that was built so that if there was an explosion, the blast would go into the mountainside to keep it contained. Before entering this plant, everyone had to place their ID badges in a reinforced concrete bunker outside of the plant. This was done because, if there was ever an explosion, no one would ever be able to figure out who was inside as they would be in millions of pieces. Again, I learned it is safety first and always. Again, the lesson was reinforced- that production plants can be very dangerous places and must be treated with the utmost care and respect for everyone's safety.

My last college job was inventorying supermarkets, where I learned that some jobs can be very boring. Still, you need to know what you have to make sense of the business.

With such great parents and this sound-loving background, I developed and refined some helpful traits for the future, which would be good for everyone.

The traits are a boundless information absorption needs to be driven by relentless enthusiasm in an organized penetrating mind supported by a need for defined, focused outcomes, and instilled with a desire to do the right things and have an indomitable spirit to try lots of things and keep going. These traits are good for everyone to have and use.

Chapter IV

School Years

Things got interesting in grammar school when I was picked for the male lead in my first grade play and kissed my leading lady. Never in my life did I think decades later, I would be in movies and TV shows.

With Dad, Aunt Mary, and My Cousins

In the eighth grade, probably because I was a big kid, I was selected to be a sergeant for the school crossing guards. As a kid, I grew at an amazing rate. To everyone's surprise, I never got any taller than six feet, the height I was in the eighth grade.

Since I was one of the tallest kids in grade school, I was put on the basketball team. From that experience, I learned the lesson that being big is no good if you are not very coordinated, so after that my basketball play was limited to playgrounds.

By the time I went to high school, I learned some coordination and was fortunate to get into a great high school where I started on the football team and threw the discus and the shot put for the track team. It was then I appreciated the need to keep fit and active, or you do not survive nor succeed. I was both a good student as well as playing on the school sports teams. A real benefit was to be able to fit in with the nerds as well as the jocks. I learned to speak publicly by serving as a lector in church at the school, finished as President of my class as a senior and was awarded a New York State scholarship to college.

In high school, I only learned two things from my English teacher. One was that there is no such thing as good writing, only good rewriting. Unless gifted with perfect writing skills, the first draft is only a start and needs to be gone over several times. I did this with this note, and it is still not as good as it should be. Also, in writing and speaking, work from an outline to provide organization, ensure inclusion and, most important, offer brevity. The only other thing was that almost all adverbs end in "ly."

I also learned from the Christian Brothers never to lie but you must only tell everything to the Lord.

While in high school and college- Although I had a New York State scholarship for college, it only partially covered costs, so I had to earn some more money. I had nine jobs, as I mentioned earlier. These included delivering groceries, selling clothing, installing and disconnecting telephones, driving a big Telephone Company in heavy Manhattan traffic, inventorying supermarkets, working in the electrical engineering lab at college, the concession stands at Orchard Beach, at the Flushing Meadows Ice Rink where the World's Fairs were held, and unloading mail for the Pennsylvania Railroad under Penn Station. I worked in two of the three most dangerous neighborhoods in NYC, which were the South Bronx and Harlem in Manhattan and never had any problems. However, I did see a lot of crime, violence, drug activity and bizarre things.

I believe everyone should have the opportunity to have a lot of jobs early in life to see what the world is like and learn basic skills, including getting along with others.

Since I was a very big kid in high school, a friend of mine asked why I did not play on the football team and talked me into joining. The team was not spectacular, but the friendships, camaraderie and fun were great.

I like football for a lot of reasons, including that it is great preparation for life. Everyone has a specific role with attendant duties, and only when everyone executes as they should does the team succeed. I learned that people make all the difference and had some of the best times of my life with the team.

I also developed the habit of exercising, which I have done every day except when I take an overnight flight. That only counts as one day since I did not sleep in a proper bed. I have had amazing health and learned while working after college that the keys are exercise, keeping a proper weight, eating fruits and vegetables, keeping away from substance abuse, and getting a good night's sleep. The secret to a good night's sleep is always going to bed tired.

At a college in Manhattan, I really took to chemistry and the physical sciences. I got hooked on chemistry as a kid after seeing a "Mister Wizard" show on chemistry. I found chemistry came very easy to me as all you had to do was think like an electron. So, I majored in Chemical Engineering in college and, as a freshman, started on our football team that only lost one game. I was lucky enough to score a touchdown as a defensive end by recovering a fumble in the end zone. *Sometimes, you get lucky, but you must be in the right place for the benefit.*

I was social director for my fraternity, which won the interfraternity football championship and was secretary of the interfraternity council. The best descriptor of our fraternity is “The Delta’s In Animal House.” There was one big difference - *while we partied hard, almost everyone had good grades.*

I was on the dean's academic advisory committee and was elected Engineering Representative for the Manhattan student government. I am happy to report that I achieved my college goal, which was to do as little work as possible and keep at least a “B’ average. Chemical engineers are very smart people, but like me, they need to learn about people, write clearly and succinctly and speak well. There is a phrase I like that sums this up – chemical engineers could rule the world if they could only speak, write, and deal with people.

For the summer after my junior year, I had an engineering project in Rochester for Eastman Kodak. As I mentioned earlier, I got drenched with nitric acid, and the equipment I was studying exploded. When the silver nitrate that we worked with got on my skin, the skin turned black when I went into the sunlight. This led me to conclude I was not meant for plant work.

When I was finishing up in Manhattan, one of my professors wanted me to go to Princeton to get a Ph.D. in chemical engineering, and he would make sure I got in. I spent a day at Princeton with a recent Manhattan alumnus in the Princeton doctoral program. He said how great it was to work hard late into the night as well as on Saturdays and Sundays. This was not what I wanted to do, so further higher education was not on the table for me at that time.

After college with a few years of working, I went to Harvard Business School (HBS) for a diploma. I found education was the most important benefit. At HBS we read, analyzed, and discussed in class about a thousand cases. The one that remains most prominent in my mind is "Interviews with Godfrey." A professor spoke with Godfrey (a pseudonym) every few years during his long and successful career. The case ends with Godfrey as chairman of his very large and very successful company as he contemplates his company's succession planning and what he will do after he retires. For me, there are three very important lessons- time goes by too fast, the need to enjoy the journey and the fact that you must be aware that nothing lasts forever. You must think about what is next, no matter how successful you are.

I recall Professor Ted Levitt telling us, "You do not have to be right but persuasive and must be sure no one can prove you wrong." Another way of saying this is a quote from Desiderius Erasmus – "in the land of the blind, the one-eyed man is king." My favorite piece of wisdom from Professor Levitt was that "the secret to success is to be lucky, and that cannot be taught; what we can teach is how to keep from being unlucky." I learned from my finance professor that control is more important than ownership. I had the privilege of having Professor Porter for a class before he became a business legend and likely helped me to quickly size up situations.

There was a course called WOC- Written and Oral Communications that provided three great learning lessons. You were given a case to analyze and submit a written solution limited to 1000 words or less to ensure brevity. The case was given at 6 *pm* on Friday. It was due at 6 pm Saturday night, and if it was late, the receiving basket was removed. Any papers not in the basket lost credit to ensure timelessness. Lastly, there was a preferred format, which included starting out with the situation, going through the data, and reasoning to get to the solution and then relating how this dealt with the question to ensure a good logically persuasive flow.

I also learned from another professor that the secret to success is "focus and detail- you must focus on what is important yet only to the appropriate level of detail." And I will always remember the great line from Professor Kotter, "Power is always relative and always changing."

I took the weekend off, stopping schoolwork at 6 pm Friday and did not start my homework until 6 pm Sunday. My only exception was to do the WOC assignments during the weekend time, as I had no choice. Sometimes, I wonder about this as I missed honors by one course grade each year. With these two higher grades, I might have been a "Baker Scholar," the school's highest academic achievement. In life, there are decisions and tradeoffs, and this was one of mine.

One thing I learned about myself was that I am not at all creative. However, I have acquired the ability to see opportunities among the myriad of ideas that other creative people generate and then bring good ones to reality. No doubt this comes from a thirst for experience and getting a lot of it.

Chapter V

Critical Thinking

Even at this point in my life, I learned not to trust the media but to look at the contents with a discerning eye. We do look to the newspapers, the internet, and television for information about the world. We want to find interesting and entertaining material. Of great importance is acquiring useful information to understand the situation around us. We need this information to help us lead our lives and make decisions that affect us, our families, our friends, our businesses, our country and even the rest of the world in some way.

We must process information with a healthy dose of skepticism. We should subject what we learn to a critical review process. The reason for this is what we get is neither completely true, nor fully accurate or even useful for several reasons. Therefore, we need to examine all information we find for at least the following nine distortions to have any hope of getting the story straight, acquiring the information we want and need as well and not wasting our time.

These distortions we must constantly be aware of are- biased lenses, linear thinking, extraordinary emphasis, personal focus, wasteful fluff, extreme obsession, negativity fear, deadline pressure, and limited expertise.

This is what to watch out for:

Bias Lenses - No matter what anyone says, they have a background, and this creates a biased view that is often propagated. Identify the bias and evaluate its merit or risk being taken in by it. This lens issue is particularly dangerous since we also have a view, and these can also fuzzy things up further.

Linear Thinking- In life, there are actions that we may be able to control, but there are events that we cannot control. Most stories delve into the future and, for simplicity, follow one or only a few paths through an almost infinite number of acts and events. Therefore, the specific conclusion is almost certainly wrong based on probabilities. We must consider the other possibilities or be blinded by many likely outcomes.

Extraordinary Emphasis - Communications vehicles crave our attention for their own purposes, which often means more followership likely to exert their bias and probably make more money. Humans have a questioning mind, and we find the extraordinary more curious. However, it may be useless, irrelevant, unlikely, or incorrect.

Personal Focus- We find people interesting, so often, stories focus on a personal situation that we can identify with or be curious about. There may be minor with little useful information. This also may serve to distract us from the big picture or the important rather than satisfy the need to get it right.

Wasteful Fluff- Almost every message has a target length, often more than needed. Also, stories begin with something to get attention that may or may not be relevant or useful. Of course, there are extra facts, details, or extraneous information to use in the allotted space. We need to gloss over this to avoid wasted time or to avoid veering to unnecessary tangents.

Extreme Obsession– Most people go about their lives doing routine things, and life is a compilation of many of these pretty ordinary actions by lots of people. The communication media usually goes after the most extreme depravity, success, failure, inconceivability, sensational etc. This is not normal or most common and needs to be understood and calibrated in this light.

Negativity Fear - Going back to early human life, we learned better to be safe than sorry and not be eaten by a lion or poisoned by bad food or water. That is why we have an ingrained orientation towards avoiding risks and rewarding this avoidance.

This is often called loss aversion. Therefore, we get communications that push up the negative. Unfortunately, it works to get our attention but is not necessarily helpful.

Deadlines Pressure – Life has deadlines, and all communications are done under time pressure. This is true if for no other reason than our lifetimes are limited because we only live so long. Therefore, the story we get is incomplete, and undoubtedly, corners are cut to make the deadline.

Limited Expertise – This is the greatest folly as no one knows everything, and many times, what we know is not correct and certainly is incomplete. Therefore, while the communicator may know something, they do not know everything. Even if they did know everything today, new facts and information may change what is true later.

There may be no right answer, but there are many wrong answers and incorrect interpretations. There are many ways to confuse, distract and waste our time and energy. This brief explanation will not make someone omniscient or clairvoyant but is intended to help their skepticism, vision, perceptions, comprehension and understanding. The goal is to help get the useful message clearer and in a more efficient way without the unnecessary.

Chapter VI

In the USA

In the USA- I have been to all 50 states, with a home in seven states and lived overseas also. In my 16 relocations, I made the equivalent of a trip around the world. My domestic travels have allowed me to go to Death Valley in summer, the North Slope of Alaska in winter, Mt. Rushmore in spring, and New England in fall. I had the pleasure of seeing Old Faithful, the Seatle Space Needle, the Saint Louis Arch, Niagara Falls, plus the Hoover, and Grand Coolie dams, Washington DC, and most everything in New York, Philadelphia, Boston, Houston, Los Angeles, and London.

I walked a portion of the Lewis and Clark trail. I stayed at some of the best places, including the Plaza in New York, the Breakers in Palm Beach, Indian Wells in Palm Springs, St Francis in San Francisco, Brown Place in Denver, Princess hotels in Bermuda and Scottsdale, Peabody in Memphis with a side trip to Graceland, Bonaventure in Los Angeles, Mansion Del Rio in San Antonio, Union League in Philadelphia, Venetian in Las Vegas, the Okura in Japan, Schloss Kronenberg in Germany, The Oakley Court Hotel in Windsor England where Dracula and the Curse of Frankenstein were filmed.

There were also many Ritz Carlton, Fairmont's (including The Empress on Vancouver Island and The Chateau on Lake Louise), Renaissance, Four Seasons with a month at the hotel in Santa Barbara, Peninsula in Hong Kong, and many others.

Being born and raised in New York, I enjoyed all that the "Big Apple" had to offer all four times I lived there, including working at Rockefeller Center, going to St Patrick's Cathedral, dinner at "Windows of the World" on top of the original World Trade Center. I ran and bicycled in Central Park and visited the Statue of Liberty, Ellis Island, Coney Island, Catskills, and the Empire State Building. I once rang in the New Year with the wild people in Times Square. I visited Grant's Tomb near where I worked one of my summers with the New York Telephone Company.

I had lunch inside the Federal Reserve, where they keep the gold, went to the New York Athletic Club, and paid my respects at Ground Zero. Near where I worked in Rockefeller Center, I ate at the Rainbow Room and snuck into the NBC commissary for lunch. Once, I was a guest for lunch in the founder's room of the Metropolitan Museum of Art and went to see the United Nations building. Later, with the boys at Christmas, we would go to see the amazing model train collection in the basement of the Citicorp building, the big Christmas tree in Rockefeller Center and visit the FAO Schwarz store to see all the toys.

New York City

Later in life, I twice went on the floor of the New York Stock Exchange on Wall Street. My greatest stock exchange experience arose from being a director of American Lithium when we listed on NASDAQ. The board started the trading session with our pictures projected on their several-story building above Times Square.

I enjoyed seeing the dogs at the Westminster Kennel Club show at Madison Square Garden. I loved visiting the Cloisters Museum on the Hudson at the northern tip of Manhattan, and this started my fascination with castles. I found the famous "Tapestry of the Unicorns" compelling. In my later travels, I visited dozens of castles in Europe and Asia. A dinner cruise around Manhattan was a real treat and I spent time in the summer at Hamptons. While working in Rochester, New York, for the summer of 1969, I drove to see Niagara Falls the year the American Falls were closed for maintenance, but the Canadian Falls were flowing beautifully.

I was delighted to get a pass to watch the Jets game from the playing field sidelines. A friend got us seats a few rows behind the goal for a Ranger Hockey game. In those days, the glass was not that high, and the players got into a fight, went over the glass landed within arm's reach.

My first professional job with Exxon had me based in Philadelphia, selling chemicals in Pennsylvania, Delaware, Maryland, New Jersey, and Virginia. This sales role allowed me to start my travels, which haven't yet stopped. I visited my customer Mc Cormick with headquarters in the Baltimore Inner Harbor with a Pacific Island village in the lobby. Another customer invited me to join him and go to Atlantic City to attend a court hearing for an employment-related case. As strange as it sounds, once at ARCO, we had a controllers meeting in Atlantic City in a casino.

Later on in life, I went on the aircraft carrier John F. Kennedy when it was in for overhaul at the Philadelphia Navy Yard, a submarine when it was in the Delaware River waterfront park, and visited the U. S. Capital, Smithsonian, FBI laboratory, Attorney General's personal office and viewed his private upstairs bedroom, Washington Monument, Annapolis, and saw the city on foot and from a dinner cruise on the Potomac River.

On a Virginia trip, I went to the Shenandoah Valley, Charlottesville, and Appomattox Court House (where Lee surrendered to Grant) and went to a tobacco curing warehouse.

Many years later, in the U.S. Japan Partnership forum, I had dinner with the Japanese ambassador at the Japanese embassy in Washinton on the fiftieth anniversary of the Pearl Harbor bombing. I had the pleasure of going to a dinner party at the house of Pamela Harrison. I remember talking to Tom Foley, the then-speaker of the House of Representatives, in front of a painting and hearing him say, I can't believe she could pay that much for this painting! I fully agreed with him.

Once, at a cocktail party, I saw a distinguished-looking man across the room with his zipper opened. I walked over to him, stood in front of him and said, "I do not want to upset or embarrass you, but your zipper is open." He was appreciative, and this started my friendship with the vice chairman of one of the largest accounting companies in the world.

During the many times I lived in the Philadelphia area, I saw Independence Hall, the boat regatta on the Schuylkill, the Liberty Bell, Valley Forge Park, attended the reenactment of Washington Crossing of Delaware and went to the Amish country.

I was a member of the Franklyn Institute and the Zoo. With the company, I had a sales dinner meeting at the Franklyn Institute and one at the Art Museum.

I looked at the William Penn Statue on top of city hall from my office. I always knew what time it was as I could look across at the big clock on the City Hall Tower. I once worked only 100 yards from the Liberty Bell and Independence Hall. I saw Pennsbury Manner did "The Rocky Run" from south Philadelphia to the Art Museum. I went to Asbury Park and Wildwood, vacationed in Cape May, and skied in the Pocono mountains.

With my ARCO roles in Philadelphia, I had the company box at the stadium to use for basketball games, circus, rodeo, and lots of other fun events. I went to the Philadelphia Mint, once had a season package to the Philadelphia Philharmonic, and enjoyed the great musical performances. I had a chance to take in a Phillies World Series game and a 76ers-Celtics championship game. I rode on the trams in Pittsburgh and later the Angels flight in Los Angeles. One of the most interesting things I did was to play Santa for my son Jon's nursery school. Little did he know he was really on daddy's lap.

When we returned from Los Angeles to Yardley in 1988 with our two Irish wolfhounds, we bought a house that had a very sophisticated alarm system with motion detectors. By that time, Dillon, the big male, was up to 200 pounds, and Kate, his sister, the female, was 150 pounds. We could never use the alarm system as the dogs were so large that they kept setting off the alarms when we were away. Nonetheless, it did not matter as any burglar that ever went into the house would never come out alive. The motto for Irish wolfhounds is "gentle when stroked yet fierce when provoked."

Chauncie, My First Irish Wolfhound

When I lived in Boston, I visited Lexington, Concord, Old North Church, and Bunker Hill. I got to visit Plymouth Plantation and Plymouth Rock a bit later. Had the chance to go on the USS Constitution (Old Ironsides) I did a Duck Boat trip down the Charles River, saw Salem, and an auto assembly plant plus a jet engine plant.

I lived nearby and saw the house where John Kennedy lived. I knew someone who did spotting for the local TV station. I got to use his outstanding seats in the Boston Garden to see the Celtics basketball and Foxboro the see the Patriots football.

I traveled around Harvard Yard when I attended business school and, years later, took a picture of my son Jon next to the John Harvard statue. This statue of John Harvard is not actually John Harvard. Few people know this, and no one really seems to care anyway.

I believe the drivers in Boston are the strangest in the world. In NYC, when the light turns red, cars go right through it. In Los Angeles, when the light turns red, everyone stops and makes sure that they do not stop in a crosswalk. Generally, around the country, people follow the traffic rules.

None of these rules seem to apply in Massachusetts. One person stops at a light, another one goes through it, someone else backs up, and yet another may make an illegal turn. We lived on a corner with a one-way street. There were so many accidents, including people going the wrong way, that I had the police on the speed dial. It happened so often could make calls to the police in my sleep. When I left Massachusetts and entered Connecticut, I pulled over and kissed the ground as I was so glad that I made it out of the state alive.

While living in Houston, I walked on the San Jacinto battlefield, went to the rodeo, traveled by boat down the Houston Ship Channel and had many trips to San Antonio and the Alamo. I once had my business team meeting in a luxury suite at the Astrodome for an Astro baseball game. I went to a football game in the Astrodome to see the Philadelphia Eagles beat the Houston Oilers, as their football team was called in those days.

I took in the Budweiser Brewery tour, Johnson Space Center, Galveston Island and more chemical plants and refineries than I can count. My neighbor was friends with Farrah Faucet, and I got a kick out of seeing the girls in the neighborhood get excited when Farrah came to visit.

Chapter VII

Living in California

During the three times I lived in the Los Angeles area, I did all the LA stuff, including Disneyland as well as Disney World and EPCOT Center in Florida, Universal Studios, Knott's Berry Farm, and the Hollywood Bowl several times.

We went to football games at the Coliseum and the Rams $6B SoFi stadium. LA has two of the best auto museums in the world, the Peterson and the Nethercutt Museum. I enjoyed visiting both a few times.

I lived close to and visited Magic Mountain in Valencia and nearby Vasquez Rocks. The rocks come out of the ground almost sideways. This is where the Jetsons were filmed.

While Manager of Operations Analysis for ARCO, I made a trip to Alaska to see the Alaska pipeline and the port of Valdez. I stayed at the North Slope when it was 40 degrees below zero to examine the drilling and equipment.

When we moved to the Los Angeles area for the first time in 1986, our second Irish Wolfhound soon after passed away. So, we got a new puppy. We wanted a big, playful, furry beast to play with the family. The Irish wolfhound puppy we got was the offspring of a grand champion, and we had to agree to show him in competitions. As it turned out, he won the best puppy at the Beverly Hills Kennell Club show that year. When he grew up, he lost his show qualities and remained the big, playful, furry family pet we were seeking.

Living in Valencia, I visited the "Oak of the golden dream," the tree that, in lore, is where the California Gold Rush began. Before living in Valencia, I lived in Westlake Village and went to nearby Malibu Creek Park to see where MASH was filmed.

Tana and I had a good time on a hot air balloon ride over our home in Valencia and landed at the local hospital, which caused quite a stir. Near where we lived was Pico Canyon, this was the site of the first oil production in the USA in 1855; it came from a natural oil seep. This was a few years before the famous Drake Well in Pennsylvania in 1859. Tana and I had the pleasure of eating at the top 10 restaurants in LA.

We attended a fundraising dinner at the Wildlife Waystation somewhat nearby. After dinner, I had a chance to get within petting distance of a Bengal Tiger out of a cage with a picture to remember the event. These tigers are so much more awesome up close and in person than in pictures or movies.

With a Chemical Society group, we had a tour of the San Andres fault and straddled the fault. Fortunately, there was no earthquake then, as my feet would be 30 feet apart in a fraction of a second if this was the Big One. I was advised by the seismologist that Los Angeles can not have an 8.2 earthquake. We have a side slip fault not a dip slip fault and this does not generate enough energy for that big of an earthquake . With my hiking buddies, I hiked up almost all the local mountains several times, including San Gregorio, San Jacinto, Cucamonga, Baldy, Wilson, and many others.

On several occasions, I visited the Griffith Park Observatory and, on one occasion, went into the exhibit that simulated being in an 8.2 earthquake. I was glad I never experienced a big one.

I was in my office on the 42nd floor of the ARCO tower during the Whitter Earthquake and got thrown over my desk, yet I landed safely without a bruise. Better than taking in several Lakers basketball and Kings hockey games, a friend worked for the owner of the Raiders when they were in LA and got me great seats at the Coliseum for the game and an invitation to the player's dinner after the game.

The Cowboys had their summer camp near my house in Westlake Village, and my sons James and Michael attended the player's dinner at the end of camp. My third son, Jon, came along a few years later. I got my picture with Coach Tom Landry, and the boys got all the player's autographs. After my fourth move to Philadelphia, I converted to an Eagles fan.

I did a lot in the Los Angeles area- Tana and I did a trail ride at Will Rodgers Park overlooking the Pacific and in Griffith Park. We watched polo matches at Will Rodgers park also. I went to the Greystone Mansion in Beverly Hills a few times, including once for a wedding. I got to go up into the control tower at LAX and view Edwards Airforce Base from its control tower. Through a friend, I got invited to a private viewing room to see the performance at the House of Blues. I went to the Comedy Factory and the Jay Leno show on another occasion.

I went to Malibu and Santa Barbra, had lunch at the Getty in Los Angeles, and Malibu had high tea at Huntington, visited Mono Lake and Lake Tahoe and skied on the local mountains.

We spent time in Catalina and made a few trips to the Channel Islands. On one boat ride, a photographer took pictures of James and Michael that appeared in an article about the islands in Sunset magazine.

When the basketball teams flew commercial, I was on a flight from LA to San Antonio with the Lakers. When I stood among the players, I felt like a child. The best part was I sat next to Coach Pat Reilly. When I asked why he was in coach and the players were in the first class, he said, "They have longer legs." Many years later, at a Gonzaga game in Malibu, my wife Tana also had the pleasure of sitting next to Coach Reilly with me by her side.

In 2023, Tana and I went Skiing in mid-summer at Mammoth Mountain on July 18. We visited four of the Hawaiian Islands, helicoptered over Kilauea, saw the place where Captain Cook landed and climbed up to Haleakala. On trips to the lake house in Idaho got to see Glacier National Park. Went to Vandenberg as I always wanted to see a rocket launch and it was loud.

In Yellowstone Park, on top of Mount Shasta, and in a park near my home in Valencia, there is something they all have in common. They all have uncontrolled toxic hydrocarbons being released into the atmosphere.

If these locations weren't natural, they likely could be superfund sites. This displays the incongruity of accepting what is natural as good and man-made things as a problem. The naturally produced Botulism Toxin and Anthrax are considered some of the most toxic substances on earth yet perfectly natural.

I had the opportunity to visit 7 of the 21 missions in California. I also went to the Rose Parade and the Rose Bowl Game on New Year's Day with my son Jon. Tana and I had a dinner cruise of LA Harbor. Once, I took Tana on a gondola ride around the LA harbor. We had dinner at the Queen Mary in Long Beach for a Guide Dogs fundraiser and another dinner at Rancho Santa Monica, the home of the first owner of the original Rancho Santa Monica. Once, got to take the boys to the opening day game of the Dodgers.

I did go to the two presidential libraries in the area for Nixon and Reagan and, on a trip to Little Rock, Arkansas, visited the Clinton Library and sat in the President's chair, which had a higher back than the others in the recreation of the Presidential White House conference room. I watched the Grand Prix in Long Beach, saw Skid Row in Seattle, and did a Duck Boat tour of the lakes of Seattle and the Charles River in Boston. I did get to see Mount Rushmore, the Crazy Horse Monument, the General Custer battlefield, and, of course, the Wall Drug Store. I got to see the Boeing aircraft plant, the Homestake Mine, and the Badlands of South Dakota.

Later, during a trip east, I spent a day in Thomas Edison's labs in West Orange, New Jersey and had the privilege of being photographed in his office, where so many amazing discoveries were conceived.

During my life I went to a lot of zoos, including the Bronx Zoo, where I got to ride a camel. Central Park Zoo in New York, the Zoos in Boston, Philadelphia, San Deigo, Houston, and Santa Barbara, plus Frankford in Germany and Sidney in Australia, and a lot of aquariums, including Boston, Long Beach, Philadelphia, and Monterey. I saw The Great Lakes and the Great Salt Lake.I went down to San Deigo to visit the Zoo, Legoland, Sea World, the Palm Springs Arial tram, and Tijuana, Mexico. Further north in California, I saw Hearst Castle, Moro Rock, the wine country, Coyte Tower, Fisherman's Warf, and Alcatraz. I went to the top of California to see some redwoods and do a strategic analysis of the business for Palco, the largest redwood producer in the world.

On trips to Las Vegas, Tana and I caught the Blue Man Group, Celine Dion, Osmond's and Circ De Soile. Also, Tana and I did the gondola ride on the lower level inside the Venetian.

From a California development activity, I received a set of commemorative cufflinks from Governor Gray Davis, who I did not like. I sent them back to the next California Governor, Arnold Schwarzenegger, and he sent me a set of his official cufflinks, which I kept.

More than just visiting some of the places, I cycled over the Golden Gate Bridge, rafted down the Grand Canyon, and did skeet shooting at a private ranch in the canyon. On another occasion, I hiked across the canyon, which is almost the length of a marathon, walked up to Diamond Head in Hawaii and hiked up to Half Dome in Yosemite National Park, helicoptered over Kilauea Volcano, and parasailed in Puerto Vallarta. I walked up to the Hollywood sign, marched in the New York Saint Patrick's Day Parade, and walked up to the Grand Canyon of the Pacific in Hawaii.

I attended the Eagle's 2018 Super Bowl victory in Minneapolis and, with James and Jon saw perhaps the greatest Super Bowl ever in Phoenix in 2023. Unfortunately, the Eagles lost; I never spent so much money to feel so miserable. My wife Tana is from Spokane and is a big Gonzaga fan. We saw Gonzaga almost win the Collegiate Basketball National Championship in Phoenix in 2017. After those setbacks, I am never going to another big game in Phoenix, again.

Jon & James at the 2023 Super Bowl

I flew the X15 rocket plane and F111 simulator at Edwards Air Force base in the Mojave Desert, plus my son Jon and I both flew trainer planes over the Pacific Ocean. I rafted in California, Colorado, New York, and Costa Rica, did the drop from the Stratosphere tower in Las Vegas, windsurfed and hang glided in Los Angeles, and became a certified scuba diver in college.

While at the North Slope of Alaska, I got to sit in the co-pilot's seat to see the oil fields with the outside temperature of a frosty 40 degrees below zero. I rowed my boat on Lake Onderdonk, where my parents bought their retirement home in New York State and canoed, sailed, and jet skied on Priest Lake in Idaho while at our summer cabin.

Even more exciting and for a bigger rush, I hiked up Mt. Whitney and Mount Shasta, ran the Valencia marathon and then the next 20 half marathons, did more than a dozen Spokane Bloomsday 12K runs, several other 10k's, did a Skydive over Perris California, watched a rocket launch at Vandenberg, drove the Empire Railroad train and a race car at Willow Springs Raceway. I rafted down and helicoptered into the Grand Canyon. I skied down from the top of Park City. I won a NASTAR Silver medal in the slalom at Breckenridge, Colorado. I did a small ski jump at Mammoth Mountain with a picture to prove it.

Medal Collection

In Arizona, I walked inside a meteor crater. I helicoptered over the jungles in Indonesia and over Dodgers Stadium in Los Angeles, low enough to see the game. We flew between the buildings just like in the movies. I even got to set off the dynamite to blow up a section of the Borax mine in the Mojave desert .

I made several trips around the world and traveled to all the continents except Antarctica. My longest trip was a 27,000-mile trip around Asia in a week.

Chapter VIII

Travels Around the Globe

In the Americas, I saw Bouchard Gardens on Victoria Island, stayed at Lake Louise, walked on a glacier, rode a hydrofoil down the Saint Laurence seaway, hiked up Mount Real in Montreal and stood on the triple point of North America where the water drains down to the Atlantic, Pacific, and Arctic oceans. I traveled on the International Loop from our cabin at Priest Lake in Idaho to Canada and back.

With James, Michael & Jon, we toured a coffee plantation in Costa Rica, and zip-lined on a private island. We had a canopy tour of the rain forest with a side trip to the Arenal Volcano to eat in a nearby restaurant to watch the lava flow down the mountain. I took in Glacier National Park on a visit to Montana.

I walked up a pyramid in Mexico and, went to Our Lady of Guadalupe Cathedral in Mexico City, scuba dove while on vacation in Bermuda and in the ocean near my house growing up. I was invited by a friend who taught a course on major global infrastructure projects to join his class for a detailed tour of the Panama Canal, meet with the people who ran the Canal and see closely the 100+-year-old equipment that makes it work.

In Columbia went to the Salt Cathedral and the Museum De Oro, rode horses in Argentina, went to the Atacama Desert and had the best barbecue of my life at a ranch near Salta, Argentina. In Rio De Janeiro, I saw the Statue of Christ the Redeemer and visited San Paulo.

On a trip to our mine in Peru, I stayed at Lake Titicaca, visited Machu Picchu, and stayed in the Eternal Valley of the Incas. Saw a few plantations, including a pineapple plantation in Hawaii, a palm oil plantation in Malaysia and a coffee plantation in Costa Rica. At work in Alaska, I saw the start of the Iditarod in Anchorage. I flew over the glacier to visit the Trans Alaska Pipeline terminus in Valdez.

When in the UK, I had the privilege to live in a huge manor house called "Pyrford Place" on the Wey River, surrounded by a golf course and a large horse farm.

Pyrford Place, Surrey, UK

On the other side of the river was Wisley Gardens, one of the most famous gardens in England, which I visited on several occasions.

The manor house had a long driveway with electronic gates to enter the property and our own fox, peacock, and frog pond. I am grateful I did not have to pay for these accommodations as they were included in my secondment package along with a BMW and a lot of other great benefits.

On my many later trips, I visited Wales, Scotland, Runnymede, Stratford on Avon, Stone Henge, Buckingham Castle, Royal Stables, #10 Downing Street, Hyde Park, Trafalgar Square and sat on Hadrian's wall. I visited the Castle of Dover and went down into the tunnels underneath used by Churchill as wartime headquarters. I went to dozens of castles, including Hampton Court, Windsor, Hever, Warwick, Edenborough and many others.

While in England I took a course in dealing with difficult customers. The key is not to get agitated but to figure out what they want. Sometimes, they only want someone to complain to. So, you listen to them, they cool down, and everyone is happy.

I saw two original copies of the Magna Carta plus the Crown Jewels, went to the Glyndebourne Opera Festival, Cartier Polo Cup championship, crewed on a sailboat at the regatta in Cowles, the largest sailing race in the world, went to the English rugby and Wimbledon tennis championships.

I also visited Hastings, where William the Conquer took over England in 1066. With the boys, we went to Edinburgh and Loch Ness but could not find the famous monster

While at the Royal Naval Observatory at Greenwich, I stood on the Prime Meridian. I had trips to the Roman city of Bath for a company meeting and to show the city to my sister. I went to some West End plays as well as plays in New York and Los Angeles. In New York, I once took the boys to the play "Cats" with a front-row seat. One of the cats came down to play with my son James during the performance. Later, James was in Cats for a school play.

I attended lunch at the House of Lords in London and dinner with Prince Philip at the Royal Chartered Accountants meeting. I visited several important houses of worship, including the Canterbury Cathedral, Salsbury Cathedral, St. George's Chapel in Windsor Castle, and Westminster Abby. With the boys, we boys visited Stratford on Avon and watched a falconry exhibition.

I had the pleasure of taking Tana to high tea at the Ritz and my sister Gerry to the Savoy. I enjoyed a dinner river cruise on the Thames with Tana as we watched the fireworks going off when we went under Tower Bridge.

In Europe and Asia – Although purchased in the USA, during my first of many trips to Europe, I picked up my Triumph sports car at the factory in Coventry, England. I got to drive around Europe before shipping it back home. When it broke down in France, the mechanic asked the color, and I said, "French blue," to which he replied, "Of course, we are in France."

I visited a lot of countries, including well-known places like Red Square, Saint Basil Cathedral, Clock Tower in Prague, The Great Wall of China, Forbidden City, Sidney Opera house, Eifel Tower, Taj Mahal, Mad King Ludwig's Castle in Bavaria, rode a train on the Rhine River to Heidelberg Castle and saw the Petronas Towers in Malaysia, Fremantle Prison near Perth where the English convicts were sent, the Sydney zoo to see Koala's up close and personal, plus Perth, Sidney Tower, Tokyo Tower, and Kalgoorlie. This is the location of Australia's first gold mine.

Taj Mahal

On my trips to France, I drove my car on the Chunnel train under the English Channel and, on another occasion, took the hovercraft on the English Channel to enjoy Paris and the French countryside.

I had the pleasure of having one of my worldwide meetings at a French cooking school in Ville St Paul near Paris. As a guest at the Peninsula hotel in Kowloon, I was transported from the airport in their Rolles Royce and visited The Peak in Hong Kong. I spent more than a month in both France and Germany during my many visits.

When I went to Normandy, I was in awe at the difficulty for the brave soldiers to storm the beaches on D-Day and scale the high cliffs while under tremendous enemy fire. Seeing the neighboring cemetery and all the grave markers of the fallen heroes is overwhelming.

I took the bullet train in Japan, stayed at a South African game park, rode on an elephant's neck in Thailand, skied in the shadow of the Matterhorn, was in Ireland on St Patrick's day, spent time in Paris, and Foss Sur Mere, Rome, Milan, and Florence (where I bought Tana the only blue Cameo I ever saw from a store on the Ponte De Vecchio), went through the Cave of Drack in Majorca, spent time in Brussels & Bruges, Amsterdam & Rotterdam, Moscow & St Petersburg, Monaco, Prague, Stockholm, Vienna, Copenhagen.

I traveled around Germany trying to track down my pre-1823 heritage but was unsuccessful, even with the help of a genealogist. I once had a sales meeting at the Zug Spritzer, the highest mountain in Germany.

I had dinner at The Palace in Vienna and had Kobe beef in Kobe, Japan, fed the revered deer in Nara, and visited Osaka Castle. I did eat blowfish once in Japan. Japan is the only country where I would eat this fish. Got to visit Switzerland, Sweeden, Denmark, the Czech Republic, Belgium, and Ireland.

I have been to Abu Dhabi and Dubai on trips to Singapore and India. Once, I spent a few weeks in Australia taking a company public and had an apartment overlooking Sydney Harbor. While there, I ran over the Sydney Habor Bridge a few times, saw the Governor's Mansion in the Sydney Tower, and attended a performance at the famous Sydney Opera House. In all, I went to more than forty countries. I saw firsthand the slums in Calcutta and in South Africa.

I studied at INSEAD in Fontainebleau, France. I walked over to see the Castle, ran around the Imperial Palace in Tokyo and the Tokyo Tower, and saw the temples in Kyoto & Nara and lots of castles and temples all around the world. I even had a chance to have some suits made while in Seoul, Korea, on one of my visits there.

Mount Kilimanjaro

A lot more strenuous, I climbed Mt Kilimanjaro, Mt Shasta, and with my oldest son James, Mount Fuji to see the sun rise over the land of the rising sun. With the Three boys, we rafted in Costa Rica, and I once ran through a Typhoon in Taiwan.

With Arco Chemical's global business management role, I had the opportunity to make round-the-world trips to our various operations. Although quite difficult, I kept these to a week. I would go East to West, then for a change, go round the world in the opposite direction. During this time, I was coaching my boys' soccer teams and would do overnight flights or whatever it took to arrive in time on Saturday mornings to coach the kids. Early in my long-haul air travels, I discovered the secret to not having time zone changes affect me. I traveled to arrive tired in the daytime and pushed myself to make it through the day until bedtime. Then, I crashed soundly asleep and woke up refreshed in the morning in this new time zone.

Of course, I always opted for the local food to fit in and experience more of the local environment. Eating food on a banana leaf in Singapore was different, and eating raw fish in a remote part of the southern Island of Japan when the fish was still moving was strange.

This litany of activities and places really helped me learn about people and the world and have a great many experiences that enhanced my approach to life, people and feeling of accomplishment.

I learned that the more experiences you can have in as many places as you can, the more you relate better and take a more expansionary view of everything. Nothing helps geography, history, and chronology than to go there and see for yourself.

Chapter IX

Starting a Corporate Career

After college, I came from a humble background, so when I graduated, I knew I did not know a lot about etiquette, finances, dressing, and legal matters. I read Emily Posts' book of etiquette, the Silvia Porter money book, Dress for Success, and the Family Legal Advisor. This got me up to speed in my four major areas of deficiency. Later, I read a recent edition of Dale Carnegie's 1937 book "How to Win Friends and Influence People," which I believe is as relevant today as when written.

I went to work for Exxon in sales. I preferred to deal with humans rather than computers at Exxon Research and Engineering. The company provided all the new sales employees with sales training that was most valuable. We learned that sales and marketing were all about profitable finding and meeting customer needs. So first, you learn the needs by asking questions going from the general to the specific. If it was a difficult discussion, it would be better to start tangentially and drive the conversation where you needed to go. When the customer said things favorable to your effort you offered a support statement. If unfavorable, ask a question to clarify and understand.

Sale jobs are more about relationships and transactions. In contrast, marketing is more about the profitability of the bigger-picture competitive situation. When agreement is reached, it is wise to restate the agreement to ensure accuracy and extract a commitment. Putting it in writing is always a good idea, if possible. I found that I related better to some of the customers, yet different ones than my predecessor. I also found that I did better with the ones that I related to better. *The takeaway is better relationships make for better results.*

When I started working, I had bad teeth with big spaces in front and packed in too tight in the back, causing lots of cavities. The other problem with the big spaces in my front teeth was I learned not to smile. Unfortunately, people often took this as unfriendly. Then someone said to me why don't you do some enamel bonding to close the spaces which I did for not much money, and I learned to smile. Now, with several crowns and implants, I have good-looking teeth. A good smile does help, just like it says in the legendary book "How to Win Friends and Influence People." This takeaway is don't hide or ignore problems, physical or otherwise, as there may be a simple, easy way to deal with them if you are open to listening and change.

I learned from a personality assessment that I was an ENTJ-Extravert, Intuitive, Thinking and Judging. This one is referred to as the "commander."

There are 16 combinations, and none are necessarily better or perfect. But some are better in certain circumstances and roles. Fortunately, my personality type fits in with my life's direction. However, if the personality type is poorly fit, things may not go as planned or well.

I also learned the difference between abrasiveness and assertiveness. Abrasiveness is aggressive behavior, including threats and accusations. Whereas assertiveness is dealing nicely but firmly with someone, listening but not caving in and looking for all the arguments and resources to get your way. Sometimes, abrasiveness is appropriate, but it is wise to always start with assertiveness and only move to abrasiveness if necessary.

After attending HBS, I learned from Professor Levitt a bit more about sales. A good salesman is someone who can successfully execute the marketing plan. In my many later sales and marketing management role I found that the biggest salesman problem was taking too much and not listening enough. Another thing I realized is -- to learn about yourself, do not ask as you will get a biased answer. In behavioral experiments, the subjects are almost never told the real purpose, as it would bias the results. So, how does one get answers about yourself? Listen, observe, and ask only tangentially related questions and often, the true answers will emerge.

I had a boss and colleagues who gave me a good deal of sound advice. A great way to start a conversation is with an honest complement and a question. The complement starts you off on a good note, and the question causes the client to think and respond. If you do not show up five minutes early, you are late. My boss also taught me if you are on business, dress at least as well as the customer or in the same manner. I once worked in a clothing store in a tough South Bronx neighborhood and learned a little about clothes for working-class people.

Nonetheless, since I came from a modest background, I never learned much about dressing for professional roles. So, I read a great book "Dress for Success," and this got me up to speed. A most important take away was- a good fit on a less valuable garment was more important than a poor fitting expensive garment. Also, I learned at the end of the sales call, always leave something to follow up on to begin the next visit. When the discussion turns to the weather, it's time to go. Lastly and most importantly, when you get the answer you want, or the order, say thanks and leave before they change their mind.

In the early 1970s, when I worked for Exxon, it was the largest company in the world with enormous resources. Nonetheless, their philosophy was "We can do anything, but we cannot do everything."

This is some good advice for everyone to keep in mind when taking on a lot of divergent activities.

I was awarded a Teagle Foundation fellowship to attend the Harvard Business School. To attend, I took a leave from Exxon and was able to work at the Bayway Refinery between semesters. I loved driving around the refinery among all the big pieces of equipment but preferred to work outside the gates to travel and meet new people.

After Harvard, Rohm and Haas, a Philadelphia-based chemical company a hundred yards from Independence Hall, asked me to join to do financial work. I really wanted to return to Exxon to use my HBS education, which focused on international business, finance, and control. Unfortunately, Exxon wanted me, as a technical guy, to go into operations. So, unfortunately, we had to part company.

I saw Independence Hall from the Rohm & Haas building, where I worked, overlooking Independence Mall. My time with the company was only a few years, and I did well and was given an award for superior performance while there.

Once, when given a difficult assignment, I said to the controller that this would be very hard. He said, "If it was easy, I would have asked someone else to do it." At R&H, I learned from the controller that after you get the answer, you must be able to explain it to others in a simple manner to be effective. If you can't do this, you have not mastered the issue and do not fully understand it clearly.

I also learned an important lesson at R&H when I did an $80 M financing. For legal documents, the name Rohm & Haas is not the same as Rohm and Haas, the legal company name. Therefore, regarding contracts and financing, the wording needs to be exact.

Rohm & Haas was once one of the most profitable and rapidly growing chemical companies. This sense of enablement led them to move into the fibers business by building on a small toehold in this field. The diversification was a disaster, causing the company to lose ~450 million dollars and take on lots of debt. This reminds me of the Exxon story – "we cannot do everything," as R&H learned at a great cost. This also reminds me of the quote from Virgil: "We cannot do all things." The other lesson is that just because you are successful in one area, you cannot assume you will be successful in another.

At R&H, I attended their assessment center to measure employee's potential for advancement. The assessor said, "he exudes confidence," and I was first on the high potential list. Since the company was struggling then and opportunities were unavailable, I had to move on.

Chapter X

AWorld of Opportunity

A friend of mine referred me to a recruiter, which resulted in an offer to join Oxirane in Princeton. They were growing so fast and so profitable that the opportunities were amazing.

The moral of the story is to work for a profitable growing company if the opportunity presents itself. The analogy is not to go for the money but to go for the opportunities, and the money will come.

At Oxirane, a subsidiary of Atlantic Richfield (ARCO) I worked on the campus of Princeton University to do some planning. I spent 14 years with the ARCO organization, getting 8 promotions, becoming the youngest corporate vice president of Arco Chemical Company at that time when I was 39, ultimately managing two different billion-dollar global businesses and making the company a lot of money.

At ARCO in Los Angeles, I did the operations analysis for most of the $25B global company. Early in my first business manager role, I finally learned to delegate. Although I could do many of the tasks better than my staff, I can't do everything.

The lesson is when something comes up, find someone else to do it and help them do it well. Professor Levitt at HBS had another saying I incorporated: "A good manager should serve as the first assistant to your subordinate."

In Los Angeles, as manager of operations analysis, I had analysts to help me with the hard work. I got to do things like attend important meetings and fly around the country with the EVP in his personal jet. The downside of this is you are like a waiter at a party; you are at the event, but you are not having as much fun as the guests.

One day, a female analyst in my department advised me she was pregnant and needed a maternity leave. After I congratulated her, I said, you need to find someone to fill in for you while you are away. She found another woman who was a good replacement and was happy to have a high-profile job in corporate, even if only as a temporary assignment. After giving birth, this female analyst returned and continued to do excellent work.

When I got a big promotion and had to move back to Philadelphia, I was asked about my replacement. I said don't replace me; instead, promote this women. She was promoted and quickly moved up the ranks, eventually becoming CEO of a Fortune 500 company. I think the moral of this story is that a competent, motivated, and diligent woman can be both a good mother and a great executive.

Once, in one of my many business analysis roles, I had to report some awful financial results. The president of the chemical company was really giving me a hard time about this bad news. Finally, I said to him- look, I did not do this; I am only reporting on what happened. He accepted my comment without any more grief directed at me and, most importantly, did not shoot the messenger.

In my operating roles, I developed new products, processes, and business relationships. When I became a business manager, the company thought I would be more effective by smoothing out some of my rough edges. Reluctantly, I went to "charm school "and it was most valuable. I learned not to pay much attention to what people said. **All that counts is what they do**. Also, many times, the best response is no response. People do not argue with a rock as the rock does not care and doesn't respond.

The other big lesson I learned at Charm School was the importance of silence. There was an interactive session about something, and after a considerable time, there were two competing arguments. Not making progress, someone called for a vote, and I did not vote as still thinking this over. As it turned out, there was a tie, and everyone looked to me for the decision. The moral of the story is sometimes you can have more power by saying nothing. I learned from a great boss at ARCO that in life, one should "work hard and play hard" to be happy and accomplished.

When I was a product manager for styrene, I got to know Jon Huntsman, and I loaned him $10 million of styrene to help him make his first acquisition. This was followed by many more successes. Later, he decided to buy Texaco's chemical company with a lot of borrowed money, and the financial offering statement advised that he may not be able to service the debt.

No sooner than this Texaco deal was finalized, the price of their biggest product went through the proverbial roof, and they made a lot of cash. Eventually, Jon built a world-class chemical company and became a billionaire.

Jon was a smart, shrewd businessman who took big risks. He was also one of the luckiest people I ever met, and that also surely helped him succeed.

In the mid-1980s, Atlantic Richfield, the parent company of the chemical company, decided to separate the top-performing businesses from the less successful ones. The resulting new entity, comprising the less successful businesses, was named Lyondell and was established as a standalone company. The business unit under my management was divided into two parts, with one remaining under Arco Chemicals and the other becoming part of Lyondell. These pieces were added to other existing businesses, and I was out of a job with nothing to do for a month. People tended to go by my office quietly or stay away, believing that I was going out the door.

What they did not know was that, early on, the president called me up to his office and said he would be reorganizing. Since I was so versatile, I would be the last piece of the puzzle. Eventually, I became the business manager for the company's "crown jewel" business.

My varied background in different areas of the company, with financial, technical, and commercial skills, paid off handsomely. *Diversification, flexibility, and a varied skill set can be quite valuable, it was for me.* The Ironic ending was that after a few years, Lyondell did well and bought Arco Chemicals. *So, the other moral is-- it is not over even when it seems over.*

ARCO was big on training, and annual objectives included a training goal. One teaching was called "get to the point." In essence one should state the conclusion or most important item first and then go over supporting information and next on into the details. The communications should look like a Christmas tree- start at the top with the top ornament and go down and branch out. Another program was about behavior. I will never forget the notion of ritualization. You are no smarter or better the minute before you get a diploma, yet only after the commencement ceremony are you a respected graduate with a degree.

Humans receive more stimuli than the mind can handle. So, the body prioritizes and sends only the most important information needed to deal with events at that time. If your foot hurts and then a lion comes charging at you, the foot pain is subordinated to the need to save your life. It is like that with information about the world.

We can only deal with so much at one time. To measure the importance of events, you need to measure the fraction of time or effort devoted to a topic or issue, not the absolute amount. Lastly, one must not forget that what we know consists of what is in our head as well as all the information we have ready access to, including people, books, reference materials, the internet, and what we see, feel, smell, hear and taste.

We are a lot more knowledgeable than we are aware and a lot smarter than in the past, but not as smart as we can be in the future.

One of the most interesting calls I ever got at Arco Chemicals was from the Senior VP's secretary. She said there was a guy on the phone who was going to come by to kill her boss, my senior VP, and could I could speak with him, which I did. With a calm manner and a discerning listening ear, I found out what was agitation him and surprisingly was able to deal this this problem. In the end, he apologized for his bad behavior. I gladly accepted the sincerity and was happy there was no violence. Also, this senior VP was one of my big supporters, and I would have hated to lose him.

I got to Los Angeles because I had to get my ticket at ARCO corporate headquarters to move up in the organization. I traveled from Philadelphia to Los Angeles to interview for a senior corporate position.

I was amazed when, late on a Friday afternoon during my last interview of the day, I asked when a decision would be made. "The controller said I was the only candidate. You can start on Monday."

While I was in Philadelphia for the second time with ARCO, I once hosted a Russian delegation to Philadelphia. I was given a "freedom dollar," which was made of recycled metal from rockets that were destroyed under an ABM treaty.

I worked on setting up the Initial Public Offering (IPO) of Arco Chemical, the largest up to that time in the history of the New York Stock Exchange. While managing a major transaction, I had the use of one of the company's G2 airplanes for a week, which was a lot of fun.

I founded the ARCO Chemical Toastmasters chapter. Everyone who aspires to a serious position must master the art of public speaking. A new top management took over the Chemical Company, and politics ended my rising career with a golden handshake. A postscript is a few years later, when Lyondell bought Arco Chemical Company, the top management that gave me the handshake was replaced. I was not sad at all.

Later in life, I learned, not surprisingly, that I was achievement oriented and the people who succeed in large companies are either political or affiliative.

After ARCO I set out to do something different with three objectives- stay in Yardley, get a senior management role, and do no worse financially than I did before.

The former president of the Chemical Company asked me to join his new company, which was on the prowl to buy chemical-related businesses. I passed this up in my quest for a role with an established company. As it turned out, after a few years, they made several good acquisitions, eventually sold the company for a lot of money.

All the original team made millions of dollars. *The moral of this story is to stay with your friends.*

Another job offer I had was to run a 100-person consulting company. Not knowing much about consulting, I spoke to a few knowledgeable people about how consulting businesses work and learned *three things to know.*

First- this is the only business where all your assets go out the door at night, and you hope they come back the next day.

Second- there are only four roles- finders who bring in the business, binders who close the deals, minders who oversee the work and grinders who do the grunt work.

Third and most importantly, you only get to eat what you catch.

There were several other opportunities to run some smaller companies where the owner and founder were ready to phase out of the business. I found out that when the day of reckoning comes, they never want to give up. None of these roles were ever filled.

To achieve these three objectives took a lot longer than I ever imagined. Although eventually, I joined Hercules in an executive role as Vice President of Planning did not relocate and made a lot more money.

I had some really nice things said about me-by-me ARCO bosses, including. When I became a low-level business manager, in a meeting, the CEO said, "I do not know what Ben does, but I know he does it very well." ***Takeaway- do a good job and you can get noticed.***

At 11am, the president asked to have a complete presentation on the subject by 1pm, and my boss said, "I have to go to a lunch meeting, do something I know will be great." ***Takeaway- be flexible and resilient.***

Another employee named Ben said to me the EVP was firing questions so fast he could not say anything. I called the EVP to say your secretary called the wrong Ben. I think you were looking for me. Then he said, "That makes sense. You would not take so long to answer my questions." ***Takeaway- a good reputation helps.***

Later, I had job opportunities to run a few private companies, and a Texas owner gave me one of the best compliments I got in my life. In an interview for his CEO position, the owner said about me in this role, "You are like bringing a gun to a knife fight." ***Takeaway- demonstrate your capabilities.***

I was deposed in an ARCO litigation and on other occasions later in my career. I was educated in how to deal with depositions. First and foremost, do not answer until your attorney gives you the OK, as the attorney may have many reasons why the question should not be answered. Also, only briefly answer the question and offer no more information. For example, if asked- do you know the time the answer is yes or no, not 2PM. There are only five possible answers- yes, no, I do not know, I do not understand the question, and please repeat the question. Once, I spent two days being grilled by a few attorneys in a deposition before they finally gave up and released me. I guess I was taught well, and it helped.

The whole goal of these depositions is to find an opening and dive in as far as they can to find something. Lastly, when answering questions, take your time, think, and take the same amount of time to answer all questions. If you answer some questions fast and others slower, someone may think you are lying or making things up when you take longer.

My last chemical-related business was Hercules, where I prepared the company's strategic plan and a lot of other activities After that role, I became CEO of its Global Environmental Solutions company with a secret security clearance to take rockets apart for the government. I also served as managing director for the Alliant Power Sources Center which was the largest producer of reserve batteries in the world to supply the U.S. Military needs. When Hercules asked for a reference about my ability to do the job, the chairman of a company, who knew me well, said, "Ben can do anything he sets his mind to," and I got the job. This is the kind of reference that really closes the deal.

Vice president of planning for Hercules was the most interesting, demanding, and challenging job I ever had. The reason was I had to do three jobs simultaneously. I directed the development of the company's strategic plan, managed, and cleaned up a few businesses that were going to be sold and did deals involving our companies in Australia, Canada, Brazil, India, and Japan, as well as the USA.

I did some media training at Hercules and learned the answer technique used by politicians. It is called the ABC method. First, acknowledge the question to show you were paying attention. Then, use a bridging statement to move the discussion to the point you wanted to make. Finally, you communicate what you want.

The sad part of this ABC training is that most people never realize you ducked the question and said something else instead. The other important point is never to acknowledge a negative question or statement. Apparently, Richard Nixon never learned this because he said, "I'm not a crook," which was dumb. When asked or accused of something bad, you say something positive instead. Such statements could be, we are honest and honorable; we follow the laws, and I am insulted by your accusations. Also, do not speculate. If you do not know something, say so and follow up with us- we are gathering the information and do not want to engage in unfounded speculation. We will get back to you when we have the facts.

Lastly, never lie as you will probably get caught, and often, the cover-up is what gets you in the most trouble, as you can learn from Richard Nixon and Bill Clinton.

I was asked to head up Alliant Techsystems Power Source Center, which had a research project to develop what the company believed was going to be the best lithium battery technology. When the CEO asked if Ben could commercialize this new technology, the CFO told him, "Certainly, but be ready if there is anything wrong. He will find it very fast." I did take the challenge, and after careful evaluation, the project ended abruptly. So, just because something looks good, there are a lot of things that can go wrong between research and production for profitable sales.

Out of the blue, with no mining experience, I was recruited to Rio Tinto's Borax company with a large market share to become the CEO when the current CEO retired. Hercules offered me a considerable number of options to go to Minneapolis and help restructure Alliant Techsystems. This was the company we merged our aerospace businesses into and kept a big ownership interest. I chose to go back to the sunny weather in southern California. Sadly, I forfeited options that would later be worth millions of dollars.

The Borax CEO wanted a business guy like himself to lead the company. Running businesses with large market shares, like I did at ARCO, requires a special and different skill set. To be successful, you must optimize the total market, including the competition, and not chase market share or price. It is a chess game, not checkers!

The other thing I learned in the past running these kinds of businesses is that you may always be watched, every meeting you attend will be known, all your calls, correspondence, and expenses can be discovered, and everything you do or say may wind up in the newspapers or worse in a courtroom.

Sometimes, simple solutions are the best. The Borax product was white crystals that came out on black rubber roller belts to go into storage. Several customers complained about black specks in the product.

This black spec problem did not affect their production but was a source of concern. The brilliant solution was to use white belts, and then no one could see the white flecks in a white product, and everyone was happy. While at Borax, I had time to do two executive programs at Stanford and had lots more world travel. I polished my communication skills at the Buckley School of Public Speaking. I was reminded that when speaking to a large audience, what you do is more important than what you say. Also, use fewer words but choose words with more impact.

I was the Chief Commercial Officer for Borax, and while there, I could not get the twenty-mule team to run, but at least I did get them to trot. On my watch, we globalized the organization and built the company's worldwide market share to 44% while increasing profit margins. Although I had opportunities to go to London and Australia with Rio, I was done moving. My days of moving were over, and I chose to stay put.

I once went to attend a negotiating course at Stamford, and the CEO said to me, "You can teach the course." Even though I had a lot of negotiating experience, we can never learn enough about negotiating better, and in many ways is what life is all about.

The best negotiator I ever met was someone who never said no. He would say- yes with, yes if, yes when. I believe this is a powerful way to agree and yet disagree at the same time. It also pointed out a route to an agreement.

To negotiate well, you need to understand what is going on behind the scenes. I learned to focus on the people first before worrying about the deal. Without the ability to understand and relate to the people you are negotiating with, you cannot secure the best deal for both parties. It Is always wise to bring another person along as it is hard to listen and talk at the same time. One person listens, and one person talks.

I believe almost all disagreements are not about the issue in contention. Behind every disagreement are beliefs, values, assumptions, and expectations. So, one must try to discover these fundamentals to have any chance of agreement. Never forget that the people you are negotiating with must save face, and there may be subsequent negotiations later. Ethics do not necessarily help in negotiations. Ethics refers to a set of beliefs and standards. However, they may not be moral, correct, good, or sound and, therefore, may not be useful to advance the task at hand.

In my many supervisory roles I found most people want to do good but often do not know what is expected. It is critical early on to set expectations, or if you are the employee, to get clear on what is required to succeed. When giving performance reviews, it is good to start with something positive to get their attention. Then, deliver any negative items and close with an action plan to remediate the problem. Always remember the person is not bad, but the behaviors that led to failures are, and they must change to meet expectations. Sometimes, this is called the sandwich approach, which sounds trivial, but it works- positives, problems and then solutions.

I learned to not only look at the next opportunity because when considering a new role, one must think about what you will do, who you will do it with and what opportunities can emerge from the move to determine if it is worthwhile.

I also learned later in life my management style was cerebral rather than emotional. While this is fine, sometimes one needs to be emotional to relate to or validate someone else's feelings and situation.

When Rio Tinto, the parent company, picked a mining guy for the top slot, it was time for me to move on and do something more interesting. By the time I brought my big company work to a close, I was able to double my salary every five years for more than 25 years.

Through the Borax relationship, I was elected director for KCET, the largest public television station in the West. I found the total divergence from everything I had done before most stimulating. Being on the board gave me the opportunity to meet some interesting people who were also very well-known, very rich and quite nice.

I had the opportunity to get to know Huell Howser, a well-known and beloved TV personality.

While at lunch with Huell, a man came up to him and said, "You are Huell Howser." Huell was nice to him, and then the guy left happy. I asked Huell about people coming up to him in public places. He said that the best thing for him is for someone to acknowledge recognition and not make any fuss. The worst is for a beautiful young lady to say to him, "My mother really likes you a lot."

Mike, Jon & James at the Mine

On one of their many visit to LA, my three sons, James, Michael, and Jon, had the opportunity to tour the TV station, including the studios and broadcasting facilities. We also went to Hearst Castle, Universal Studios, Edwards Airforce Base, and the Borax mine in the Mojave Desert. They looked a bit out of place at the mine because they were still children wearing big hard hats and standing on the enormous mining trucks.

Chapter XI

Home in Yardley, Pennsylvania

Before and between the times I moved to LA, I had a lot of good things happen during my three times in Yardley. Around the time of the bicentennial, I bought my first house. The address of this corner house was 1706 Yardley Road. I learned the house across the street was 1800. I spoke to the postmaster and asked who had the numbers between 1706 and 1800 and was advised no one, so they were available. I had my house number changed to 1776 Yardley Road, and no one forgot my address. The moral of the story is to make things you want to be remembered memorable, even if that requires a bit of change.

At 34, I won a bet by losing 90 pounds in nine months, going from 265 pounds to 175 pounds. With that much weight off, I felt like Superman, and everything physical was easy for a while. I wish everyone could have that experience, as it was great. After losing all this weight, I took up running to keep it off and did 6-7 miles a few times a week. Much later in life at the age of 49, I decided to do the Valencia Marathon, having never run more than 7 miles at a time in my life. After 17 or 18 miles, I pooped but persevered, finished with a reasonable time, got my t-shirt, and vowed never to run a marathon again.

I still exercised every day unless I was on an overnight flight, and running was a lot easier than with all the extra pounds.

Living just across the Delaware River from Trenton, I had many visits to the New Jersey State capital at Trenton to see the capital and the museums. My youngest son, Jon, wanted me to coach his soccer team. There was only one problem, I did not know anything about soccer and at age 40, I had never kicked a soccer ball. So, I signed up for the adult soccer league to learn the game. The league had a random draw for players on the teams. As it turned out, I wound up on a team with most of the best players. With these guys, I was able to play a lot because we almost always had big leads, and I could learn from them and make mistakes without any pressure. I had the privilege of playing on this undefeated team and got good enough to be a respectable player. The lesson is when you are around great people it is safe and easy to learn and win.

I was an AYSO division director once and coached 25 soccer teams for my three boys, including a coed team. To coach, I had to go to training and learned that with young kids, you must keep them busy, or they will get into trouble. Also, with kids and well as adults, don't tell them what they are doing wrong; show them the right way to do something, or they will do the wrong thing over again. Hence the need to prepare practices well before showing up.

Once, I had a team that I coached that included my youngest son, Jon, and we had many great players. We had a goalie that could stop a truck or a swarm of bees. The kids played hard, spread out, listened to the coach, stayed in their lanes, and played defense. Usually, we were up by a few goals, and I could get everyone to play no matter what their ability. Once, I got so overconfident that I allowed the weaker players in too long, and we could not make up the last one-goal deficit. That was the only game we lost that year. However, I take comfort in the line, "It is not who wins or who loses but how you play the game." Nonetheless, I still wish we had won and had a perfect season.

James, & Michael with Dancer, & Stretch

One of the greatest compliments anyone ever paid me was when the referee did not show up, and the other coach asked me to referee our game with his team. When I ruled a controversial call for a goal against our team, I got a lot of our kids and parents mad at me. Still, fortunately, our team won, with my assistant coach doing a great job. We had three horses; one was a barrel racer, and if you pulled backward on the reigns, Dancer went backward. I had five Irish Wolf Hounds, which gave the boys rides by hanging on their tails. I was elected chairman of the Institute for Cooperation in Environmental Management.

Chapter XII

Keys to Leadership

I did learn something about leadership, and with decades of international and top management roles in multiple industries, I had the opportunity to learn about leadership. I also had the opportunity to know many individuals called "leaders." What I found out is that leaders are not gifted, brilliant, extraordinary individuals with multitudes of dedicated, ardent followers. This is only the myth of leadership. Leadership is not real; what is real is followership, and that is the key. Followership makes all the difference, and it is derived from transactional benefits.

While lots of people talk about leadership, and there is an untold number of books and stories about this subject, I believe they all have the story backward. The truth is-- it is all about followership. People only follow leaders because there is some benefit in doing so. When the benefit ceases, what was identified as leadership vanishes. Leadership only works because it offers benefits, and nothing more mystical or ethereal than that.

To understand why this is true, let's consider what leadership is, which often stems from charisma. I would submit charisma (or leadership) is a combination of status, vision, attractiveness, power, authority, knowledge, and trust.

The only reason this matters is these attributes provide something to the followers that they want. Status can provide recognition to the follower. Likewise, vision gives the follower purpose. Continuing along, we see attractiveness offers validation; power can get the follower resources. Authority offers protection, knowledge offers information, and trust can yield friendship. This is not an exclusive or complete listing, and there are many overlaps with each other and a few more in different ways.

So, how can one acquire and exhibit leadership? The answer lies in providing benefits just like any other business transaction. So, a great leader is not a larger-than-life demigod whom individuals crave to follow. The real secret is followership, which stems from providing benefits to the followers. In simple terms, the leader is the supplier, and the follower is the customer.

When the product (leadership) on offer does not satisfy the customer, there is no followership and, therefore, no leadership. When the price for the offering does not measure up to the benefit, the power of the perceived leader ceases. Then, the followers move on to the next provider of wanted benefits, and then this person is called a leader. So, if you want to be a leader, always think about satisfying those that you want to have along with you.

One can be a leader by listening to the customers (followers) and understanding their needs. Then, provide what is wanted and needed to the best of your ability. If you do this well, someone will call you a leader. But all you have done is to acquire followership. You can only keep this going until you are no longer willing or able to satisfy the followership obligations.

So, when you meet the followers' needs you will be called a leader. Only then do you satisfy the followers and provide the desired benefits. This is why leadership is a myth. The followers are really in charge of offering followership, and they do this only on a temporary basis at their discretion.

One other thing I learned about successful leaders, they are often their harshest critics. It is this drive to improve that propels them to succeed. The Japanese have a word for this: "kaizen," or continuous improvement. Also, in life, you can watch things happen, make things happen or let things happen to you. Depending on the circumstances, any of these three approaches may be useful in leadership. Nonetheless, in an uncertain world, the most likely way to predict the future is to make things happen. The necessary corollary is-- not to be overbearing or overly controlling, as nothing gets done except fostering bad will.

Chapter XIII

On to Entrepreneurial Activities

With adequate resources, I chose to move on to embryonic work, including buyouts, startups, and some consulting. I am certainly glad that I got into this stuff with the ability to take big risks and live comfortably, no matter how it turned out. I came close with three great deals in different areas with Champlain (optic materials), AMT II (ballistic fibers) and IMEX (commodity mineral), any one of which would have given me a multimillion-dollar payout. Although each one was on the way to closing, a different last-minute problem doomed all three of these. Fortunately, I was treated well by a few others, but you always remember the big one that got away.

I was a principal for AMT II, a buyout group in the aerospace and defense business. We were planning to acquire the Corus technology developed for the UK Ministry of Defense, which could essentially make buildings blast-proof from external explosives. I spent a week in Scunthorpe near Lincolnshire in northern England evaluating this technology, economics, and its implementation. Unfortunately, it worked too well. If an embassy or government building employed this technology and a bomb exploded outside the building, the protected building could resist the blast. Still, the overpressure would go in other directions and destroy the surrounding buildings.

The moral of this story is --- sometimes, even if the technology works perfectly, it still may not be a good business opportunity to pursue.

I became CEO of Kreido Biofuels and took the company on the stock market through a public offering. The technology was amazing and could speed up chemical reactions by an order of magnitude. Although the technology worked, and we spent about $40 million developing it, we could never get it to achieve its potential.

A friend of a friend of a friend helped me get a role teaching International Business Management at UCLA one semester. It was hard work. Even with decades of international management experience, I had to put in 3 hours of preparation for each class hour. In management roles, you are called on to be an instructor to your employees, customers, and other business-related interests. However, this is to accomplish a goal. Teaching for its own sake was not as interesting, and I was finished as a professor.

Probably the strangest assignment I worked on was to evaluate the business of Palco, the largest redwood producer in the world. I was retained by a McKinsey partner who had some ownership of the company.

I said you are a partner in the most prestigious business consulting company in the world – why do you want me? To which he replied, with your background and skill set in dominant global businesses, you are better able to do this than anyone we have.

I did some evaluation for multibillion-dollar funds like Lincolnshire, Clearlake, Tennenbaum, CVC Partners and others. My role was to do a quick evaluation to see what was there and if buying the company made any sense. It was a great learning experience analyzing many companies in my area of expertise in chemicals, energy, and materials. There were other board and advisory roles to keep active, each quite different and quite interesting and very educational.

As CEO of Potash Minerals, a publicly listed Australian company, we discovered almost a billion-ton potash resource in Utah that was believed to be the largest in the U. S. The potash resource was in San Juan County. Still, the Bureau of Land Management (BLM) office that governed most of the property was in the city of Moab, a tourist and recreational center. The county could not do enough to help us as they were dependent on farming and ranching and wanted jobs and development. The product we were after was "potash" (chemically known as potassium chloride). This is both safe to eat, used as a table salt substitute and necessary for all plant life.

The domestic market was in short supply, prices were up, and most domestic customers purchased imported potash. Mining consisted of putting hot water down a hole more than a mile down and bringing up a salt mixture of potassium chloride and sodium chloride, "table salt." The potassium was removed, and the water solution went back down to where it came from. The site was on state and federal land. The state permits took only two months, whereas, for the exact same drilling, the BLM permits took a hard two years. The approvals required from the new Obama administration eventually killed the project, after we spent $30M and the stuff is still in the ground.

I once got some sound advice from a banker that rang louder than ever- **"There is no such thing as a mining project, only a permitting project."** Almost everything we use is either grown or mined on about 1% of the land yet using that 1% for mining is extraordinarily difficult and very expensive. Everyone needs food, electronics, cars, etc. Still, there is great opposition to having domestic producers supply the minerals required to make these items.

To do start up or venture work, you need a lot of money as it is difficult and often takes a long time. Raising this money is also very hard as you need a great business opportunity and a good story.

I believe the story should answer the following twelve questions in roughly this order.

1. What is the field?
2. What is the opportunity?
3. Who are the people?
4. What is the advantage?
5. What is the proof?
6. What is the quantification?
7. What is the plan?
8. What are the projections?
9. What is the investor's return?
10. What is the exit?
11. What is offering?
12. Who should be contacted?

And should also include an appendix with important background or supporting information.

No experienced or serious investor expects things to go exactly as planned, so they know that, ultimately-- they are investing in the people.

According, they need to be convinced that this team is—

- Committed,
- Knowledgeable,
- Resilient,
- Flexible,
- Perceptive,
- Responsive,
- Reliable
- Trustworthy

And therefore, the team can deal with whatever comes along so The investors get their money back with a good return.

I am proud to match my personal investment performance with the professionals by racking up a 12% year on year increase in my IRA for more than twenty years running before I had to take mandatory withdrawals. I did this by investing in businesses and industries I knew something about but never hit the home run as I could never go all in or take the big risky bets.

Yes- there is a free lunch in investing; it is called diversification, and it works to mitigate risk. One must not confuse diversification with diversity.

Diversity is fine only if it provides a benefit such as information, flexibility, stability, understanding, relationships etc. We could get a lot of diversity by adding animals or dead people to the organization but that likely would not help and most likely would make things a lot worse.

I believe when considering any situation, there are three categories of things to keep in mind.

First, there are 8 questions to ask.

1. Who is involved?
2. Who pays?
3. Who decides?
4. Who does time help?
5. How is the decision enforced?
6. Who is the customer?
7. Who benefits?
8. What is the product?

Secondly there are some basic facts to keep in mind in working on the solution remember.

- May control actions cannot control outcomes.
- Control is more important the ownership.
- The situation depends on the perspective.
- Time to exit determines success.
- The risk depends on the individual.
- Strive to make the pie bigger.
- Everyone is different.
- Follow the money.
- Stress is personal
- Divide and conquer.
- Is this a one-off or ongoing?
- Segmentation is key.

In a group, there are competing objectives. Importantly, goals determine the process.

Third and most importantly - How do I benefit?

I later joined the advisory board for Millennial Lithium, which was sold for 400 million dollars. Then, I joined as a director for American Lithium with some of the world's largest and best-undeveloped lithium and uranium resources in our mining claims located in Nevada and Peru. While in mining, I developed a framework for what it takes to develop a mining project. It also costs lots of money.

- Rapidly growing large unmet market opportunity.
- Control over a high-grade, easily accessible ore source
- Cost-effective, environmentally sound mining and production process
- Great access to infrastructure, transportation, and markets
- Ability to secure regulatory approvals with community support
- Necessary inputs of energy, water, labor, electricity, and materials
- Management and organizational resources and capabilities to succeed

With my entrepreneurial experience and from my prior lives, I learned that there are a lot of ways to make money if you are not fortunate enough to inherit it, marry into money or win the lottery.

From my travels to Asia, Africa, and South America, I believe everyone fortunate enough to live in the USA has already won the lottery. Otherwise, to make real money, you need to leverage yourself.

There are a few ways to do this, including founding, owning, or running a company. Another way is to go into a high value-added role with an asymmetrical payoff for the top performers, such as in sports, finance, entertainment and, unfortunately, politics after you retire with a household name and lots of contacts. The third way is to do something one time that allows you to get paid over and over, such as writing a book, patenting an invention, or making something else that is used and paid for over and over, such as a movie or advertisement. Although it is too late for me, I hope this stimulates some thoughts for a reader.

All my opportunities after Rohm & Haas came about through friends and personal contacts. They introduced me to people and opportunities that I could never have found. Also, when these people vouch for you, you are validated, and the chance of getting the job is very high. **Never forget to keep in touch with friends and contacts when you are busy, as they can be amazingly helpful when you need them.**

During my quite varied career, I had the opportunity to go to more than a thousand plants, mines, laboratories, and factories around the world. I enjoyed seeing each one in person to learn something new and meet many nice people from these experiences.

I served in the mentor program for Harvard Business School students, was a mentor and advisor for entrepreneurs at the Los Angeles Cleantech Incubator, was a director for the Harvard Business School Alumni Association of Southern California and was on the Valencia Water Company citizens advisor committee. I taught a class on international business management at UCLA. In one of my companies, I won a significant lawsuit from a big law firm and got a large payout. I was once recruited to do some work for the CIA, which I declined.

In my HBS mentor role, the key thing I tried to convey to the students is to do what you like as you will enjoy it and most likely be better at it. Also, stick with your friends. It is critical to develop a simple story of who you are that fits with what you want to do. If the story does not fit this role, either change yourself or change what you want to do. Only later in my career, too late for me, I learned if you want to get ahead in a big company make friends with the person who will someday run the company and tag along.

As I mentioned before, in large companies, there are at least three types of people: affiliative, political and achievement oriented. Usually, only political, or affiliative make it to the top. Achievement-oriented people should learn and move on as likely they will only achieve their potential by running their own company or working for the board of directors and/or their friends. I only learned that I am achievement-oriented at the end of my big company career.

There is a lot written about bad people like Madoff and the bad deeds they do. I do not think they were bad at the beginning. I believe in slippery slopes. People start out to do the right thing and then face problems, so they feel the need to cut corners. Then, they must do more to recover as the hole gets deeper. After that, they are on a slippery slope, and things keep getting worse until they get caught. Then, people ask how anyone can do those awful activities. So, what is the solution? It is to keep away from the edge before you get caught on the slippery slope.

Another belief of mine related to this is that problems do not happen suddenly. I always liked John Kenneth Galbraith's statement, "All successful revolutions are the kicking in of a rotten door." The analogy of the rotten door is a good one, as situations do not fall apart suddenly, it was rotting for a while and never fixed. Then, the proverbial straw that breaks the camel's back comes along.

So, we must be aware of the rotting door and deal with it before it is too late.

I spent time with many different recruiters as a candidate for numerous positions in my career. The first thing to know is they need to get a mental picture of who you are, so make it easy and give it to them early on in a capsulized format. Second, when dealing with recruiters and others, it is better to keep the answers only as long or only a little longer than the questions. If they want more info, they will ask. I once was at dinner in a restaurant with Tana, and at the next table, I could tell someone was being interviewed for a job by a recruiter. I said to Tana he was finished and won't get the job. You could see this candidate could not stop talking and see that the recruiter was not interested in listening any more. This is good advice for company interviews or personal encounters.

The best book I ever read about dealing with recruiters is "Rites of Passage at $100,000" by John Lucht. Although in the new versions, he added $100,000 to $1,000,000, I guess this is due to inflation since the earlier version I read. If you ever want to get a critical view of your resume, show it to a recruiter, as they see thousands and can give excellent advice. It is also wise to have many recruiters as friends as I did for career advice and to help advance some of your friends that fit their needs that they will often share with a trusted source.

Chapter XIV

Life Has Uncertainty

There is a lot of uncertainty today to deal with. I lived through the Cuban Missile Crisis in 1962, the oil shock of 1973, the fall of the Berlin wall in 1989, the terrorist attacks of 2001, the global financial crisis of 2007-2008, regional wars, revolutions, border conflicts, natural disasters, and the chaotic elections of the last few years. Weighing this against what I see today, I believe there is more uncertainty and risk now than at any time in my life.

At home in the USA, we are getting more polarizing bad news than our society can handle. This is compounded by COVID fatigue with all the fear, divisiveness and distrust that goes along with it. Crime is rising, and academic achievement is falling. Just when we thought inflation was defeated, it took off, and a recession is looming. We have a dysfunctional government. Many Americans have lost faith in our leadership and democracy.

Things are not much better in Europe, with a totalitarian leader in Russia waging war and killing innocent civilians in the Ukraine. In Europe there are many more cracks with Brexit, independence movements, nationalistic disagreements, populist uprisings, energy disruptions, and money problems.

In Asia, we have a dictator for life in China arming for a global war to enslave the people of Taiwan. Next door is a North Korean leader starving his people and playing nuclear blackmail for leverage to extort the West. These issues are now causing a remilitarizing in Japan while other Asian countries pursue self-sufficiency. It seems that human trafficking and abuse are getting worse than ever.

There are a lot of global trends that also do not look good. There are more desperate fleeing refugees with no place to go. We see greater religious warfare, with innocent people being killed in the name of God. The world's instabilities have caused a setback for globalization by diminishing the benefits of trade and reducing the availability of goods. The corrupt and powerful elite destroy democracy, liberty, and economic opportunity for their citizens. If I could change anything to greatly help the world's problems, it would have term limits on leaders.

Rather than countries and people becoming more peaceful and integrated, there is more polarization, tribe mentality, and ethnic aggression fueled by more dangerous weapons.

Our society is straining as technology is moving faster than people can handle, thereby paralyzing and overwhelming the ability to respond. The population around the world is aging fast, and we are facing a situation with more takers with expensive medical bills and fewer payers to cover the costs.

Now, there are greater capabilities to make more powerful synthetic opiates that destroy too many lives.

The world and its people always overshoot and undershoot. Too often people respond to what they see right in front of their nose and not to the fundamental and the possibility of black swan highly unlikely events.

The situation is bleak, with great risk and uncertainty, but it is still not hopeless. In life, there is a lot of stress, which is the body's nonselective response to stimuli. My belief is not to let the stress get to you but channel it into productive activities and it can be released. This is not a call to panic but a wake-up call. It is time to carefully think about these problems. We must seek solutions and find people to make the world better, not worse. Then, we need to act to improve the situation, or it will get even worse with more uncertainty, risk, and problems.

Chapter XV

With Some Spare Time

With some spare time, I spent a week in Sacramento. I found the Binninger bible, which was misplaced in the California archives. The Bible was brought to America by Jacob Binninger, who was a 49er and built the first brick building in Sacramento. I was allowed to go to the artifacts warehouse to take a picture of the brick. It seems that Jacob was not my great, great grandfather. Even with the help of a genealogist, I could not go back much further in German records. Most likely, we are related to each other from way back before Germany was a country.

For some variety, I did background work in more than 25 TV programs, movies and documentaries playing a dean of a medical school, lawyers, executives, wealthy people, a policeman, and those you barely see in the background. I did get to starring role in a History Channel documentary as a newsman. I played a colonel in a CIA training film. For an episode of "Big Shot," the coach was shown staring at my picture. I was portraying his dead father.

When I first moved to the Los Angeles area, I went to Universal Studios and went on the tram around the back lot. Never did I think that 20 years later, I would be waving to people on the tram as I was going to play a senator on the set of Evan Almighty. On a few occasions I got to drive my car around Universal Studios and Warner Brothers film lot going and coming from car scenes where I drove.

On the Screen

I had the privilege to get my copy of renowned Harvard Professor Benjamine Friedman to autograph my copy of "The Moral Consequence of Economic Growth" at the home of one of his former students. I took a course in Molecular Biology, and this confirmed my belief that I like molecules but not biology.

This biology stuff is way too complicated for me as each person has thirty trillion cells, each an incredibly small and complex chemical factory. In the human body, 100 thousand proteins interact in myriads of integrated chemical reactions, many more than anyone can comprehend. I learned a lot but could not keep track of all the names and process steps.

What I do remember is that evolution only occurs when it provides benefits to organisms. Perhaps we should take that advice and change ourselves when it helps.

I took the course as I thought someday biological processes would overtake traditional chemical processing for bulk chemicals as the reactions tend to be more selective. Now, I believe this will only occur with pharmaceuticals and other high-value products as the reactions are too slow, have too many steps, are too sensitive to conditions, occur on a smaller scale and are too costly for now.

I won bronze medals in the discus and silver and bronze medals in the high jump at the California Senior Games. I penned many published editorials for the local newspaper. Even after playing tennis regularly for fifty years, I still never got very good. Since I have a lousy backhand, I sometimes switch my racket from my left hand to my right hand without even thinking. I have always felt an obligation to give blood since it did not cost me anything and could do some good for someone in need. I am happy to say I donated my sixth gallon and, thankfully, never had to ask for any back.

I received some things I never would have guessed. Through my wife Tana's father, we obtained a very small ownership in an iron ore mine in Minnesota. With him, I got to stand on the ore we were later to own a small part of.

We also received a small ownership in a very very small oil property in Michigan. From him, we got to own the family cabin on Priest Lake in Idaho, although we had to buy the land from the state at an auction. I had a plan for my life, but it never turned out the way I intended. I could never have anticipated all the opportunities and fun I would have, and I tried to take advantage of everything that life offered.

Chapter XVI

Along Came COVID

In 2018, the world was subjected to one of the worst medical catastrophes of my lifetime with fear, death and grave illness that continues. It would have been good if leaders, media, and government officials told us the truth. Wouldn't it be great if we knew everything about the coronavirus?

Based on science, we would know how it would affect all of us. With this knowledge, our leaders would have the wisdom to select the best decisions for the optimum solution based on scientific certainty. Today, we are led to believe pronouncements with statements and implications like:

"We are making decisions based on science, and therefore, it is correct and what is best."

Unfortunately, these decisions are often wrong, misleading, biased, and illogical for a myriad of reasons, including the wrong science. This misleading overconfidence is a hidden problem that is not addressed. Also, there are known unknowns which are information that we know that we do not know.

The only certainty about the coronavirus is that the data, analysis, and conclusions are highly uncertain. There is a strong likelihood that it's wrong and certainly incomplete.

What we know for sure is that there is imperfect information. Specifically, there is not enough information with perfect statistical accuracy because there is not enough perfectly accurate testing done by perfect people on all the individuals affected who are doing this with all the time they need for absolute certainty. Furthermore, from chaos theory, we know that even if we did know how the virus works, this may not yield correct answers because there are unknown unknowns in initial conditions. Accordingly, a small change to inputs will upset the otherwise perfect system. No matter how certain we are of the system and its workings, there is always uncertainty.

There is little doubt that coronavirus information is filtered by individuals who have personal biases about the problem, the solutions, and the information. Moreover, many different people are looking at different views of the situation and inevitably see different things. This is not physics with clearly defined laws. Even physics with clearly defined laws changed as Einstein modified the laws of Newton with his better knowledge and brilliant new insights.

To compound the problem, there are misleading judgments that there is an optimum solution. There is only an optimum solution if there is a clearly defined objective based on fixed rules and fully known inputs. Therefore, the optimum depends on who is defining it and not on an absolute truth. Humans are risk averse and inevitably ascribe more weight to bad outcomes than good outcomes, and this is certainly reflected in the analysis, interpretation and decisions about a nasty virus that kills a lot of people.

Although we want to keep people alive, there is a tradeoff between saving lives and economic outcomes that is glossed over by saying the approach is scientifically based. These tradeoffs inevitably incorporate value judgments based on politics, viewpoints, personal situations and at least as many considerations as there are people in the decision-making.

Humans are both illogical and logical at different times and under different circumstances. Conclusions are often presented as sound, reasoned logic based on irrefutable facts. Unfortunately- the facts, accompanying logic and decisions may or may not be correct. Certainly, the individuals involved are not always correct.

Knowing all this, what are we to do? I do not know for sure, but ***what I do know is—***

When someone says that this action is based on science, do not believe them. Think of the quote from Somerset Maughan: "The fact that a great many people believe something is no guarantee that it is true." What we need to do is to carefully look behind the decision and be very skeptical, or we will all be in trouble.

Chapter XVII

We Need Information and Energy

With enough information and energy, there is not much that cannot be accomplished.

Once upon a time, world news traveled by foot, animal, train, and ship. This took weeks or months to go significant distances and was therefore scarce and valuable. This news came in verbal, written, analog, and then digital forms. Later, electronic communication moved via telegraph, cables, and satellite, which allowed it to arrive almost instantly. As this was happening, more and more sources of news were created, including correspondents, networks, and now direct person-to-person communications. Because of all this, the range of geographic news coverage, amount of information and speed, the volume has become overwhelming. Yet, people still have a limited amount of time.

This is where we are today with an information orgy. There is too much news to deal with, and this makes it very difficult to absorb and determine its accuracy. Over the ages, the value of news has diminished as the volume and speed have grown. Furthermore, since there has been too much growth in sources of news competing for limited audience time, organizations and individuals have taken to create their own news.

It doesn't matter if this news is true or not if it gets attention. If news reports are not noticed, there would be no way to absorb the supply and secure the resources to create it. This situation is a logical outgrowth of too much supply chasing limited demand. There is a great temptation to go beyond reasonable limits to get noticed and a willingness to ignore consequences.

What do we do when faced with this information and news glut. The only solution is... *be disciplined, economical, and selective with the information we accept.* We should stop looking at and paying for this overwhelming volume either directly by paying for it or indirectly by supporting individuals, products and organizations that finance these sources. By removing this financial support, some excess sources fade away along with incorrect or unnecessary information.

Too much useless information wastes our time, misinforms, and distracts us from productive efforts. Information only has value if it educates, entertains, enriches, or enables better decisions. Just because it is cheap and available does not mean it is useful and needed. We do not need an overabundance of information. Still, we need information that meets the 'C O R O N A' test by being:

Concise, Organized, Relevant, Objective, Not sensational

and Accurate.

Information without activity is not much use. Some say that information is of no value unless it causes us to act differently. To act differently, we need technology to secure lots of cheap, abundant, safe and sound energy. Without energy, the universe ceases, and nothing gets done. We need energy to live and for the earth to function. We need energy for heating/cooling, transportation, food, communications and to make all the goods we use and to rid ourselves of the trash we do not need any longer.

With inexpensive energy technology, we can make materials in short supply or high in price goods more available. We can fulfill any concern about water shortage by recovering drinking water from the ocean. Many of our limitations and environmental issues will not be problems. If we have enough inexpensive energy, they can be dealt with. So, what do we do? Find cheap energy and use it as freely as we can. Easier said than done. The only problem is that the technology is not there yet, so we need more helpful information to gain the knowledge to create technology to make a better world based on cheap energy.

Chapter XVIII

Thinking Things Over

I did what I could and am happy with the results of my life covered in this note. They say there are three versions of a situation- what you saw and heard, what you remember and what really happened. I can honestly say this story accurately contains all three versions, including, most importantly, what really happened.

I thank the Lord for a great life and my excellent health. If He did not give these to me, the note would be a lot shorter and life a lot less enjoyable. I learned early on that life is a marathon, not a sprint. However, if you fall behind, it is hard to catch up. As Michael Phelps says, "It doesn't matter where you start but where you finish", and you must finish to succeed. There is no doubt that people matter, and the people in your life can make you a better person if you let them.

One important lesson is to consider the first "no" as a suggestion or recommendation and then try again. Remember, no does not mean forever. Things do not always work out as you want, and some bad outcomes can't be changed. Nonetheless, you can always change your attitude and actions to make the best of any unwanted outcome. Also, perhaps the most important thing in life is just showing up.

I had a boss who had a sign over his desk, which I agree with: "You miss 100% of the shots you never take". I have learned the best place to store information is in your head. It cannot get lost, is always with you, and no one gets to see it unless you let them. When confronted with adversity or a problem, one should ask, will this be important a year from now? The other question to ask is, what do you want to accomplish, and will this action advance me to this goal?

I don't subscribe to the line, "You can because you think you can," but I do believe "You can't because you think you can't." I also believe that if you aim high, you won't necessarily achieve what you set out to accomplish but likely will achieve higher than if you aim low. Another boss had a picture of a turtle over his desk with the caption, "Behold the turtle who only makes progress when he sticks his neck out." This does not recommend taking crazy risks, but it does say that- if you stay in your shell, nothing good can happen. Another important lesson I learned is to first get the facts and then deal with them as they are, not the way you want them to be. Always remember the advice from Carl Sagan… "our preferences do not determine what's true."

Once, someone asked me if I believed in UFOs, and I said yes. This stands for unidentified flying objects. Of course, things are flying around I can't identify that are not necessarily driven by green men in flying saucers.

The moral here, as Stephen Covey said in “The Seven Habits of Highly Effective People—"seek first to understand then to be understood.”

I realized that less is often more, and actions are what counts. I always liked the statement from the former Chinese leader Deng Xiaoping: “It doesn’t matter if a cat is black or white as long as it catches mice.” A favorite expression of mine is “I believe in what works,” and the lesson from the bible in Mathew 7:16 is “We shall know them by their fruits.” It is believed we have crystallized memory and fluid memory. Fluid memory is what you have when you are younger, with rapid learning, quicker processing and finding new things. Crystallized memory from past learning comes about as one gets older and doesn’t go as fast. We draw on more resident information and past learning. So, if you are not there yet, get ready to rely on crystallized learning, as fluid memory is fading, like it or not.

Although I have a few regrets, sadly, my boys did not get to grow up in the loving family environment my sister and I had. My boy’s mom and I are two very different people, and with our divorce, the boys did not have the great family life in which I grew up. Later, I married the most wonderful woman in the world. My only regret in our marriage is not having a daughter as beautiful as my wife, Tana.

In many ways, my life got better as the years progressed, and I have Tana to thank for that.

Tana and Ben

I am an eternal optimist but believe without communication, nothing is possible, and without information there can be no activity. Nonetheless, underlying every human interaction is the requirement for either hope or trust as well as resources to get anything done, even though results are always limited by capabilities. Don't ask why but ask what first. Remember, in the end how is more important, and the results are meaningless without specifics and an understanding of the consequences.

Fear causes inactivity, and there is a tendency to be overwhelmed by the present, so the past and future are discounted to the present, making outcomes overshot and undershot. Certainly, outcomes dictate subsequent actions.

In the end, hope and trust is what keeps us going or else nothing happens. We all need hope and trust for the future to bring about better outcomes.

There are some views we need to reassess.

We should reassess some of the fundamental beliefs that we harbored, including.

Thinking- *We can predict the way things will proceed.*

We are too focused on the present and believe the future will be like the past; therefore, we engage in linear thinking as change from discontinuities is constantly occurring.

Problems- Once we solve this problem, things will be fine.

We only have a limited capacity to deal with problems. As we solve one or it solves itself, the mental capacity becomes available for another one to deal with.

Communications- *If only communications could be better and faster.*

During the millennia, communications speeded up from meeting in person to ships, telegraph and wireless. Speed is no longer the criteria but the cost, amount, and value of content. We need more useful content and less irrelevant content.

Money- *We need electronic money and never have enough.*

Electronic money is already everywhere today; money is not real or tangible anyway. It is only trust for value in the future because of an enforcement mechanism to protect this claim. Money is created through enterprise and efforts not in the ether or a computer program.

Solutions- *This is the answer to our problem.*

For every problem, there are proposed solutions often incorrect, emotionally driven, too costly and judged without considering changing circumstances or the cost of being wrong. Assuming any solution is the ultimate answer is foolish.

We must always be mindful of the wisdom of Will Rogers, who said.

"It Isn't what we don't know that gives us trouble. It's what we know that isn't so."

In life, just like in poker, it does one no good to complain about the hand you were dealt --- It is what it is. The best you can do with the hand is to play what you received as well as you can. I hope this story helps a bit to enable you to play your hand better. As life goes by so fast and there are a lot of good things that happen, we should all adhere to the advice in the quote from Doug Ivester: *"Never let your memories be bigger than your dreams."*

I am an optimizer rather than a maximizer. I did a lot, but I do regret not doing as much as possible. I will keep going as I have not yet heard the fat lady sing, so hopefully, there is still more time to keep at it, get some more accomplished and have more fun. I pray someday I will hear the Lord say to me, "reasonably well done and good enough to get by generally faithful servant." As you might imagine, I am not looking forward to hearing this for a long time.

Chapter XIX

Insights from India

A few years ago, I was invited to speak at the New Frontiers in Engineering, Science and Technology (NFEST) conference in Delhi, India. When I asked Professor Kumar, a friend of mine, what I should talk about, He said, talk about anything you want. I figured that all the other speakers were going to discuss some interesting novel technology or research developments. So, I decided to go with something different. For many decades, I have been making notes on human behavior and I had a desire to share this with a wider audience. I did my talk, and I guess it was OK as they asked me to do the closing remarks summarizing the meeting, which was a great honor. The section that follows is a summary of the talk titled.

Please note in my original talk, which follows, I have put some items in parentheses and discussed a story or anecdote that is not presented here.

Behavior: Understanding it, Using it & Changing it

In the past people jokingly said that Brazil is the country of the future and always will be. Today, people are not joking when they say that India is the country of the future because the future is now.

Twenty years ago, I was traveling around India as the nation was celebrating a great milestone- fifty years of independence with a bright future still ahead. I am delighted to be here with all of you in this place at this time, with India now just about the fastest-growing large economy in the world.

I am also delighted to have the privilege to speak with you about **Behavior- understanding it, using it and changing it.**

During a long, active, and full career in international business, I have learned something about the world and the people in it. I am grateful for the opportunity to have served in 26 roles, with many in top management. I have worked in eleven different companies, overseeing operations in 25 countries. This included businesses ranging in size from millions to billions of dollars in a dozen different industries. To do this, I relocated twelve times, covering more than one trip around the world and loved every minute of this thoroughly enjoyable journey.

While going about my job, I learned something about how things work and how to affect outcomes. Probably nothing that I will talk about is new or revolutionary. I am happy to share what I have found, and it is likely you already know a lot of this but never thought much about it.

First, I will speak about how I believe the world works. From there, I will move on to talk about behavior and what we can do to affect outcomes. My contribution was to compile and organize what I saw, what I heard, what I learned and what I concluded during my career and travels. I tried to do this with a clear, concise, and comprehensive summary of key observations and conclusions. I gathered as much useful information as I could and then distilled this into essential elements.

What follows comes from decades of mistakes, observations, and learning. I hope you will find this material useful. Likely, I have captured some insights from others. Nonetheless, I am certain that the words and the organization are mine alone, and this is my original work.

Ladies and Gentlemen, I believe that this is how the world works.

First, let me begin with this thought.

"Sooner or later, common sense, reality and economics prevail, but that does not preclude reputations and fortunes from being made and lost in the interim."

Some principles govern everything.

— Time is the most precious commodity and can never be replaced (only live so long)

— No person can predict the future no matter what they say (inaccuracy of forecasts)

— Unfortunately, we do not know what we do not know (unknown unknowns)

— Overtime outcomes repeat, but people affected differ (wars, catastrophes, achievements)

— In life, we must use what we have, or we will lose it (body, mind, relationships)

— Opposites attract in magnetism but not for very long with people (divorced)

— Genius has limits, yet stupidity is unbounded (Darwin Awards)

— The more we know, the more questions we have (the frontier of knowledge)

But people matter a lot and can affect outcomes.

— We are social beings and behave accordingly (we all exist in a society)
— We are all different and view everything somewhat differently (varied backgrounds)
— We need to feel in control even though we are not (consider utilities)
— We act either because we want to or because we have to
— We fear loss more than we value gain (risks from animals)
— We are all the reference by which we measure others (smart, tall, old)
— We never know how much is enough till we know how much is too much (lose some deals)
— We should never ascribe to malice what can be explained by ignorance

We are controlled by the process of change.

— Change is the only constant thing, although it varies over time (what has not changed)

— Problems are all personal and relatively varying with time (health, family, job)

— Change is hard as it requires us to do things differently and change ourselves.

— Technology and innovation create both improvements and risks (fertilizers, nuclear, internet)

— Rules provide benefits or challenges as we deal with change (consistency vs responsiveness)

— The change will overshoot and reverse over and over (stock markets)

— Economics, stimuli, and influence work but not immediately or as anticipated (later outcomes)

— Progress is not so much about doing smart things than not doing stupid things (catastrophes)

Now, with this background, let's move on to behavior.

First, let's identify some rules that affect Behavior.

- It is not over until it is over, and even then, it may not be over (many problems reemerge)
- You must know where you are before you can know where to go (spaceship guidance)
- Progress must be measured compared to expectations, where you were & compared to others.
- Results are determined by who gets to be the judge (boss, spouse, stockholders)
- Although people can control their actions, they can only influence outcomes (ever failed)
- Indecision is a decision not to decide.
- Cannot write the script for the option that was not chosen as the world changes (unknown)
- The second problem can be worse and result from dealing with the first problem (accidents)

Then, let's talk about the Behavior of others.

— Normal people do what is best for them no matter what they say (charity)

— People follow not because of leadership but because it's good for them (self-interest)

— Look first from the other person's perspective because they will

— Begin with something positive, or others stop paying attention (performance review advice)

— Ignore what others say but watch what they do (critical-talk is easy, i.e., The Royal Society 1660)

— Do not let others make their problems your problem (the no-room story)

— Treat people as you want to be treated, then as needed, treat them as they treat you

— Useful communications can only occur if communications are understood (language)

In life, we are all selfish

"Fair is when it is good for me; unfair is when it is not."

— First, try to be nice. You can always get nasty later (red/blue training)

— Before you play the game, know the rules, the stakes, and the quitting time (keep dealing)

— You miss all the shots you do not take but do not waste your resources foolishly (football)

— Often, no response is the best response (extinguish)

— Having difficulty choosing among many good alternatives is the best problem to have

— Carefully react to problems as often overreaction creates a worse predicament (fights)

— Do not make decisions before you must but at the right time under the right circumstances

— To get results, you need a goal, a plan, resources, and a place to start (preparation)

Now, let's see if there is some general advice on Behavior. And of course, **there are some Behaviors we should adhere to ourselves.**

— Be careful of what you know as it may not be so (flat earth)
— Make it easy for others to do what you want them to do (critical- other prospective/interest)
— Being liked is a great way to get what you want (like/dislike-competent/not competent)
— Tell the truth, and you only must remember one story
— Consider who is involved, who is affected, who loses, who gains and who pays (big picture)
— Begin with the goal in mind and a close measurable milestone (today=future)
— Ask what I want to accomplish, and this action will help me get there (do this always)
— Think about how you respond and critically how this will be viewed later before acting

And a last bit of advice

"Consider the first NO as merely a suggestion or recommendation.

BUT *Use this to understand what the other party really wants.*

THEN *Find a way, if possible, to meet their real needs.*

LASTLY, *Most importantly, in a way that is good for you also."*

Please use what you like. If you disagree, I will not be offended. My interest is not to change the world or any of your opinions. My goal is to provide something that may challenge your thinking and help you realize what you already know.

I hope you can use this for some benefit and my reminder helps you improve your life, your relationships, and your decisions in some small way. I provide no guarantee other than this is how I found that things are, and it seems to make sense to me. I trust it will make sense and be useful to you in your journey.

I would like to thank Dr Kumar and the NFEST organization for allowing me this opportunity to be here with you. I look forward to the opportunity to learn from all of you now at this conference and hopefully on many future occasions.

G A Ben Binninger- January 2018

About the Author

G A Ben Binninger

G.A. Ben Binninger is an accomplished executive with a wealth of experience in leading and establishing technologically advanced process and service companies. He has successfully managed operations of various sizes, ranging from a few million dollars to global businesses exceeding a billion dollars, for world leaders such as ARCO, Hercules, Alliant Techsystems, and Rio Tinto, as well as several startup ventures.

His expertise spans mergers and acquisitions, turnarounds, and public offerings, showcasing a unique blend of global management experience, strategic positioning, technical proficiency, and financial acumen. With hands-on leadership in industries such as chemicals, energy, materials, environmental and mining, consulting, technology, and defense, Ben has led businesses for industry leaders with substantial worldwide market shares.

Ben's skill set includes negotiation of deals and transactions on a global scale, commercialization of novel technologies, and development of new products, businesses, and companies. He possesses a broad functional background encompassing sales, marketing, distribution, operations, technology, evaluation, finance, planning, and business development.

With a Master's in Business Administration from Harvard Business School (HBS) and a Bachelor of Chemical Engineering degree from Manhattan College, Ben's educational background is complemented by practical experience. He has taught international business management at UCLA, studied at Stanford University, INSEAD in France, and The Buckley School of Public Speaking.

Ben has held key leadership roles in various organizations, serving as Chief Executive Officer and Director for ASX-listed Potash Minerals, Principal in AMT II Corporation, and Chief Executive Officer and Director for Kreido Biofuels. His involvement extends to positions such as Director of American Lithium and Governance Chair, Advisory Board member for Millennial Lithium, and service on the SCV Water Citizens Committee. He has also been an advisor and mentor for the Los Angeles Cleantech Incubator (LACI).

Beyond his professional achievements, Ben has a diverse personal life, including climbing mountains such as Kilimanjaro, Whitney, and Fuji, participating in marathons and half marathons, winning medals in the discus and high jump at The California Senior Games, and engaging in extra work in TV programs and movies. He has traveled extensively and provides guidance to acquisition groups, venture funds, and growth companies. Additionally, Ben has been actively involved in nonprofit organizations, including roles as a director for The Harvard Business School Association of Southern California, KCET - Community Television of Southern California (Compensation Chair), American Defense Preparedness Association, and Chairman of the Institute for Cooperation in Environmental Management.

Made in the USA
Columbia, SC
18 April 2025

54954e87-319a-4c1d-8b9e-ce48408c0158R02